*The Myth of Christian Beginnings*

# THE MYTH
## of CHRISTIAN
## BEGINNINGS

Robert L. Wilken

**UNIVERSITY OF NOTRE DAME PRESS**
**Notre Dame, Indiana**

University of Notre Dame Press edition 1980
First published by Doubleday & Company, Inc., 1971
Reprinted with permission

**Library of Congress Cataloging in Publication Data**

Wilken, Robert Louis, 1936–
   The myth of Christian beginnings

   Reprint of the 1971 ed. published by Doubleday & Company,
Garden City, N.Y.
   1. Church history. 2. Christianity—Essence, genius, nature.
I. Title.
[BR145.2.W5 1980]    270'.09    80–11884
ISBN 0-268-01347-0
ISBN 0-268-01348-9 (pbk.)

Manufactured in the United States of America

*to Carol*
  *Always changing*
  *Ever new*

# CONTENTS

# PREFACE

What does it mean that Christianity has a history? In modern times there has been a great deal of talk about the historical character of Christianity. "Christianity is a historical religion"—so the phrase goes. Some make this claim to assert the uniqueness of the Judaeo-Christian tradition among the world's religions. Others use it to criticize traditional Christian thought patterns because they are too metaphysical or abstract and because they are thought to distort the Hebraic faith by translating it into the categories of Greek philosophy. For others, the phrase designates a particular theology about how God acts in history. Whatever the merits of calling Christianity a historical religion, I am convinced that few Christians are willing to take with complete seriousness the proposition that Christianity is indeed a historical phenomenon.

All the many ways of talking about Christianity and history overlook the most obvious characteristic of any historical phenomenon: change. This is not surprising, for if there has been a constant in the history of Christianity, it is the reluctance of the tradition to give a place to change within the Christian experience. Most Christians have been willing to say that Christianity changes in some areas but in others remains the same. There may be changes in church polity, or in morals, or even in doctrine, but the "essence" of Christianity—what Christianity really is—remains the same. Christianity itself does not change. But why should we assume that some aspects of Christianity change while others do not?

The Christian attitude toward change is reflected not only in doctrine, church polity, and morality—witness the birth control controversy within Roman Catholicism—but it can be seen most clearly in the way Christians have viewed their past. This book is a critical examination of the Christian attitude to change, as reflected in the Christian construction of the past.

My constant intellectual companions continue to be Richard John Neuhaus, pastor of St. John the Evangelist Church in Brooklyn, and Philip J. Hefner, professor of systematic theology at the Lutheran School of Theology in Chicago. The ideas in this book have been sharpened in discussions with them over the past several years, and each has read the manuscript with a keen and critical eye. I am also grateful to J. Kevin McVeigh and my assistant, Joseph Hallman, both of whom read the manuscript and made helpful suggestions. Eva Hoenig typed it with her usual enthusiasm and dispatch. During the writing, my wife, Carol, to whom this book is dedicated, never let me forget—my behavior to the contrary notwithstanding—that there are things in life more important than writing books.

Robert L. Wilken
New York
June 1970

What has been is what will be, and what has been done is what will be done; and there is nothing new under the sun. Is there a thing of which it is said, "See, this is new"? It has been already, in the ages before us.

(Ecclesiastes 1:9–10)


Remember not the former things, nor consider the things of old. Behold, I am doing a new thing; now it springs forth, do you not perceive it?

(Isaiah 43:18–19)

*The Myth of Christian Beginnings*

# CHAPTER I

## *The Use of the Past*

CHRISTIANS, like others, cultivate the memory of the past for the uses of the present. On stained-glass windows and frescoes, in sermons and schoolbooks, men and women of old—Abraham and Moses, pharaohs of Egypt and kings of Assyria, apostles and martyrs, popes and saints—stride before the Christian imagination. Abraham is a symbol of faith, Moses spoke with God on Mount Sinai and transmitted the Ten Commandments to the people of Israel, martyrs gave their lives for the faith, and saints show men a godly life. Even the deeds and misdeeds of such unlikely figures as Cyrus, king of the Persians, Naaman the Syrian, and Pontius Pilate are told again and again. The memory of the past nourishes the Christian imagination, enriching men in life and comforting them in death. Arising out of a tradition whose heroic figures are part of ancient history and whose formative events took place centuries ago, the Christian imagination is, in large measure, a historical imagination. When the Christian sings, he dreams not only of a new heaven and a new earth or of the Kingdom of God; he also dreams of the river Jordan, the dry and dusty hills of Palestine, the places where Jesus walked, and the days when apostles ruled the churches and martyrs met death in the Coliseum at Rome. To cultivate the memory of the past, Christians have developed customs, formed institutions, formulated beliefs, and, significantly, written and rewritten their own history.

Not everything from the Christian past is remembered. Like all memory, the Christian memory is selective. Instinctively, men filter past events through the experiences of the present, remembering those events that readily take on the hues and colors of the present and forgetting those that do not. Christians are as adept at forgetting the past as they are skillful at remembering it. Long centuries are forgotten; others are celebrated. Men read and reread some books of the Bible; others they ignore. The contours of memory are frequently erratic and arbitrary, following neither conventional historical standards as to what is significant nor accepted literary standards as to what is beautiful. Most Christians have never read, nor will they ever hear read, one of the grandest poems in the Hebrew Bible, the Song of Songs. Even well-educated Christians are ignorant of the several hundred years of Jewish history from the exile of the Jews in Babylonia in the fifth century B.C. to the birth of Jesus. Christian song and verse celebrate the age of the apostles, yet few hymns commemorate the giants who lived in the centuries after the apostles. The Christian memory leapfrogs over whole epochs as though they had disappeared from the historical record. Many Sunday-school children could name an apostle or two—Peter, James, John—but few would be able to name one major figure from the apostolic age in the first century to the Reformation in the sixteenth century.

Of course, not everything is worth remembering. As many dull and uninteresting people and as many prosaic and predictable events litter the Christian past as litter any other historical record. There is no reason to remember everything or to pretend that each moment, each man, and each book are equally important. In the long view, ninth-century Italy is not as significant as first-century Palestine; Ethiopia is not as significant as Germany; Dionysius, bishop of Alexandria in Egypt in the third century, is not as significant as Augustine or Thomas Aquinas or Martin Luther. Indeed, in an age of prodigious historical scholarship it is worth recalling that long and learned tomes written about second- and third-rate figures are likely to make very dull and very bad history. There is no mandate, either religious or historical, to reproduce the thought of everyone who ever lived, simply because some monk happened to make a copy of a manuscript. Historical thinking is and should be selective. In the silence of the study, many historians—at least this one—have given thanks that the monasteries of Europe and Asia have *not* preserved every book written in antiquity. Yet this is not the point. The question is rather: why do men remember what they do? What Christians remember and what they forget are not due simply to the accidents of manuscript transmission or the idiosyncrasies of Greek monks. Men remember times that are poorly documented in our sources and forget others whose sources are rich.

Men remember the past for the uses of the present. No doubt, this statement has a ring of cynicism, as though memory "exploits" the past to serve the present. Men have always misrepresented, manipulated, and falsified the past to serve their own ends. "Historical truth may be discovered by professors of history later," said Goebbels at a mass meeting in Berlin in 1942; "we are serving historical necessity."

### MEMORY AS PART OF SELF-UNDERSTANDING

Rummaging around in the historical record to buttress one's own opinion—the statesman seeking historical analogies to defend his nation's action, the politician criticizing his opponent on the basis of alleged "facts," the churchman arguing a theological point by citing authorities congenial to his views—are not the only ways men use the past. Instinctively and unconsciously, we single out certain men and events as more representative, more typical, more significant for our own past. Because we live in the present and expect to live in the future, the past takes on meaning only as it is distilled through the reality of our present and future. The memory of the past, because it is partial and selective, unravels the tangled threads of our lives and weaves them together in a symmetrical pattern. Memory is part of self-understanding and identity. Over the years, we accumulate experiences, form impressions, and construct our own story. Moments of high drama, days of joy and ecstasy, times of grief and pain, the first love, a beautiful summer, a year of turning—the extraordinary moments in our lives become the vehicles by which we understand, identify, and find our place in the world.

What memory is in the lives of individuals, history is for groups—organizations, institutions, religions, or nations. We cannot ask a nation to lie down on the psychoanalyst's couch to recall and rehearse the experience of distant days; yet the past is often more alive for a nation than it is for an individual. The way nations and religions imagine and reconstruct their pasts, the times they choose to recall as well as the events they choose to forget, the idealizing and romanticizing of whole epochs, the embellishing of seemingly insignificant events, the creation of heroic types and symbols out of unknown men, are as much a clue to a nation's self-understanding as its laws, political institutions, music, literature, or art. Men need a past, and if they do not have one they will create one to suit their purposes. A nation, like an individual, cannot bear the idea that it has no beginning and no history.

"Memory is the thread of personal identity, history of public identity," writes Richard Hofstadter. "Men who have achieved any civic existence at all must, to sustain it, have some kind of history, though it may be history that is partly mythological or simply untrue. . . . One of our early nineteenth-century promoters of canals and public works was also a promoter of historical collections because he understood with perfect clarity that there was some relation between the two. 'To visit a people who have no history,' he wrote, 'is like going into a wilderness where there are no roads to direct the traveller. . . .'"[1]

THE VISION OF AMERICA'S PAST

In the early years of this country, it seemed that, in comparison to the European nations, the United States had no history. How could Nathaniel Hawthorne make literature with so little history, Henry James once asked, when there is no sovereign, no aristocracy, no palaces, no cathedrals, no established church or clergy, no centuries-old schools and universities, no monuments? At first Americans took pride in not having a past. Instead of a past, America had a future, and this was more pleasing for the imagination to contemplate. Yet, there had to be a past. Why not Europe? All Europe, some said, was the American past, and the experiment in the new land is only the next stage in the development of European history. Eventually, however, Americans began to create their own unique past—legends, sculpture, monuments, shrines, ballads, heroes, villains.[2]

What a past it was! The Americans outdid everyone else. The new nation was unique, without peer, unparalleled in the history of mankind—the chosen people. Until the appearance of the American nation, said President Woodrow Wilson, the ". . . great body of our fellow beings have been kept under the will of men who exploited them and did not give them the full right to live and realize the purpose that God meant them to realize." The nation signified a new beginning, the settling of a virgin land unmolested by the dirty hands of previous generations, for in this people the world is about to enter a new era in which the kingdom of heaven will fully come on earth.

The conviction that the United States had a mission to redeem mankind grew out of the historical interpretation of the uniqueness of the American past. Even to this day, the belief in a "redeemer nation" shapes the self-understanding of this nation, influences its way of life, education, and culture, and even determines aspects of our foreign policy. Speaking before the United States Senate at the turn of the century, Albert J. Beveridge said, "God had not been preparing the English-speaking and Teutonic peoples for a thousand years for nothing but vain and idle self-contemplation and self-admiration. No. He has made us the master organizers of the world to establish system where chaos reigned. He has given us the spirit of progress to overwhelm the forces of reaction throughout the earth. He has made us adept in government that we may administer government among savage and senile peoples. Were it not for such a force as this the world would relapse into barbarism and night. And of all our race he has marked the American people as his chosen nation to finally lead in the redemption of the world."[3]

The nation had a right to be proud. In the space of two centuries, the small bands that had settled on the eastern shore of the new continent had tamed the land, built cities, and established universities, won independence from mighty Britain, mastered a vast continent, and founded democratic institutions unparalleled anywhere in the world. What wonders God had worked among these people in the new world!

The vision of America as a redeemer nation was a credible interpretation of the American past, even at the close of the nineteenth century. But such a heroic view of the American past demanded much forgetfulness. Americans, too, have their spells of amnesia. The other side of the American past—the exploitation and extermination of the American Indians, the devastation of the land, the rapacity and opportunism of American business, the prejudice against blacks and, paradoxically, immigrants and foreigners, the violence of American life—these men forgot, no doubt because the future promised that the dream, even if marred by some memories, could one day come true.

As recently as spring 1969, the report of the National Commission on the Causes and Prevention of Violence, in its report "Violence in America" noted how forgetfulness is characteristic of the American view of the past. "Americans have been given to a kind of historical amnesia that masks much of their turbulent past. Probably all nations share this tendency to sweeten memories of their past through collective repression, but Americans have probably magnified this process of selective recollection, owing to our historic vision of ourselves as a latter-day chosen people, a new Jerusalem."[4]

Selecting, forgetting, idealizing past events, i.e. the historical construction of the past, are as characteristic of religious groups as nations. Most English-speaking American Protestants trace their origins to the colonists who came from England in the early seventeenth century and settled at Massachusetts Bay and Plymouth. Parents, schoolteachers, clergymen have told and retold generations of children the tale of persecution and oppression in Europe and the desire of these first Americans to establish religious freedom in the new land so that men might live together peacefully, tolerating different views. Few ideas have entered so deeply into the American consciousness, whatever one's religious origins. Each year, school children listen raptly to the tale of the Pilgrims; at Thanksgiving, Americans relive the Pilgrim celebration with a festive meal, the President issues a proclamation, and the nation gives thanks for its unique inheritance. Even such a fundamental pillar of American life as the separation of church and state is widely thought to be an inheritance from the first settlers. Yet those Pilgrims never dreamed of establishing religious freedom in their colonies. Indeed, they had no idea of toleration. Citizenship and church membership were thought to be identical. In the priceless words of one early divine, "All Familists, Antinomians, Anabaptists, and other Enthusiasts shall have free liberty to keepe away from us." And another: "Tis Satan's policy to plead for an indefinite and boundless toleration. . . ." The land, however, was spacious, and men could, if they found the atmosphere confining, simply move on to form a new colony. Religious freedom grew up gradually, as the colonies learned to deal with the problems of religious diversity. Nevertheless, even after the founding of the nation, many of the original colonies, now states, maintained their earlier practice of officially recognizing one

branch of Christianity—Congregationalism, Presbyterian-
ism, or Episcopalianism—as the official, i.e. established,
religion of the state.[5]


THE MAGIC OF LEGENDS

Historians can debunk the myths about our past, they
can reinterpret the historical record and rewrite the schoolbooks, but they cannot ignore, nor easily dispel, the magic
of historical memory to mold men's lives and thoughts.
Historical memory has a life of its own. A historian looking back on the 1960s may conclude that John Kennedy
was not a great President, but for millions of Americans
who lived through the three years he was in office and experienced the shock of his assassination, the historian's
opinion may strike them as irrelevant, if not perverse.
Critical historical scholarship will refine and modify the
remembrance of those years, but the memory of the man
will be shaped as much by the impact he had during those
few brief years, as it is by the careful research of the historian.

Mircea Eliade tells of a legend in a small village in
Maramures, in Romania, in which a young suitor had
been bewitched by a fairy, and a few days before he was
to be married, the fairy threw him from a cliff. Shepherds
found the body, and when they returned it to the village,
his fiancée poured out a beautiful funeral lament. Investi-
gating the legend, a folklorist discovered that the story had
taken place only forty years earlier and that the heroine
was still alive. He spoke with her, and she described a

quite commonplace tragedy. One evening, her lover had slipped and fallen off a cliff; he was not killed instantly, but was carried to the village, where he soon died. At the funeral, the fiancée participated in the customary ritual lamentations. Popular memory had stripped the story of almost all historical authenticity in spite of the presence of the principal witness and many other villagers who were contemporaries. "When the folklorist drew the villagers' attention to the authentic version, they replied that the old woman had forgotten; that her grief had almost destroyed her mind. It was the myth that told the truth; the real story was already only a falsification."[6]

At the first Vatican Council, in 1869–70, where papal infallibility was proclaimed, some bishops protested that the historical record showed that popes were not infallible. Nevertheless, most bishops chose to dismiss the historical argument because the "construction of the past" as it lived in their communities and in the collective memory of their fellow bishops was infinitely more "real" than the pedantic jottings of a few historians.

Alfred Schutz, one of the more creative men to write on the sociology of knowledge, once wrote an essay on the problem of "reality" in Cervantes' *Don Quixote.* He posed the question of William James "Under what circumstances do we think things real?" in relation to the different worlds inhabited by the Don and by Sancho Panza. The Don lived in a world of courtly ladies, towering castles, chivalrous knights, and extraordinary events, whereas Sancho inhabited the world of the baker, the barber, and the innkeeper, a world of scrawny horses, dirty inns, and dreary villages. At first glance, Sancho seems to live in the "real" world, but if his world is compared with the physical world of rocks and trees, rivers and mountains, tables and chairs, smoke and sand, Sancho's world is seen to be only one kind of reality. For in the world of rocks and trees there are no taboos, no traditional mores or values, no well-defined roles such as barber, valet, or innkeeper. Sancho's world exists alongside of other worlds. "There exist," wrote Schutz, "several, probably an infinite number of various orders of reality, each with its own special and separate style of existence, called by James 'sub-universes.' Among them is the world of the senses or physical 'things' as experienced by common sense, which is the paramount reality; the world of science; the world of ideal relations; of 'idols of the tribe'; the supernatural worlds . . . ; the numerous worlds of individual opinion; and finally, the worlds of sheer madness and vagaries, also infinitely numerous."[7]

Men can and do create private worlds of their own imaginings, but most of the worlds we inhabit are, in the words of Peter Berger and Thomas Luckmann, "socially constructed." That is to say, we inhabit them with others. Language, law, morals, religion, accepted patterns of behavior, well-defined roles, and institutions are part of a socially constructed world created by man.

Language, for example, is a human product originating over many centuries, reflecting the creativity of countless individuals, the experience of millions of people, and the refinements brought about by constantly changing demands. Language is not "given" as part of the physical world, as are rocks and trees, vocal cords, tongue, and teeth. Nevertheless, though language originates in ourselves, it is not imaginary, it is not a dream or a fantasy. It is most definitely real, as any child learns when he begins to imitate his parents. Language presents itself to the child as "objective," and to become a part of society he must learn the language. He cannot wish it away, ignore it, or pretend it is not there. It is there and it is real.

Take another example: A young couple can repeat the words of the marriage vows in a rehearsal on a Friday evening, but they are not yet married; the next day, at the wedding, the same words mean something quite different, for after they are spoken, the couple are married. The "reality" of the marriage does not originate in, let us say, the physical relation between the couple, but in the meaning that society assigns to the wedding ceremony. Another example: A boy and a girl can walk across an American college campus holding hands; a girl and a girl can walk across the same campus holding hands; but let two boys walk across the campus holding hands!

### WHAT IS "REAL"?

Historical memory contributes to the social construction of reality. What men consider "real" or "plausible" rests, in part, on historical constructions of the past. How would a Southern Baptist congregation respond to a sermon urging them to pray to the Blessed Virgin Mary? What authority would a statement of Karl Marx have in a meet-

ing of the John Birch Society? In moving from one religious tradition to another, one discovers that what is
plausible in one community, another community rejects
out of hand. Protestant churches frequently have names
such as Christ, Redeemer, Faith, Our Savior, or Grace,
whereas Roman Catholics use names such as St. Leo,
Our Lady of Victory, St. Rose of Lima, or Immaculate
Heart. When I was a seminary student, my instructors
taught me to prefer sixteenth- and seventeenth-century
chorals over the hymns of the nineteenth century. To this
day, I catch myself looking at the date of a hymn before
choosing it for use in congregational worship.

It should be made clear that the phrase "historical construction of the past" does not mean that the historical
memories of communities are false because they are "constructed." It simply means that on the basis of the same
historical data different interpretations are possible and
arise as much out of the collective imagination of the
communities as they do out of the historical "facts." When
sociologists speak of reality as constructed, they mean that
the worlds men inhabit are the products of the men who
make them, and that they derive their reality from human
beings who continually reproduce them in their lives. To
speak of historical constructions of the past is to speak
of the way the memory of the past is formed by the experiences of a community, and kept alive as the community
reproduces these memories in its ongoing life. Someone
living outside of the community may have quite a different perception of the same historical events.

CHRISTIAN AND JEWISH VIEWS

To illustrate: Both Jew and Christian share a common history in ancient Israel, but because of the different historical experiences of the Jew and the Christian since the time of Jesus, their constructions of the past have almost nothing in common. The Christian sees the history of the ancient people of Israel as part of his history, and interprets the writings of ancient Israel as pointing to the coming of Jesus. After the death of Jesus, the Christian sees a division taking place because of the attitude of the Jews to Jesus. The Jewish Scriptures pointed to the coming of the Messiah, but when he came, the very people who looked forward to his coming did not recognize him as the Christ. Those who did, became Christians and believed that the ancient inheritance of Israel was faithfully preserved in the Christian Church and perverted within Judaism. Because Jesus was thought to be the fulfillment of Jewish hopes, Christians believed that, with the coming of Jesus, Judaism would cease to exist as a distinct religious community separate from Christianity.

Judaism did not cease to exist. Jews have been present throughout the whole course of Western history, and they have insisted that Jesus of Nazareth was not the Messiah. Ancient Israel did not come to fulfillment in Christianity. There is another religious community that claims to be the inheritor of the same tradition Christianity claims as its own. In the twentieth century, this has been dramatized by the establishment of the modern State of Israel in Palestine.

Christians have always been perplexed and troubled by the presence of Jews. If Jesus was the fulfillment of Jewish expectations, why do the Jews not embrace this Jesus? To explain this seemingly inexplicable fact, i.e. why there are still believing Jews, Christians have traditionally said that the Jews "rejected" Jesus because they were blind and hard of heart. They had the Scriptures, which spoke of him, but they were blind to their true meaning. The idea of the "rejection" of Jesus by the Jews is a theological and historical construction of the past, by Christians, to explain why there was a division between Judaism and Christianity and why each had a separate history for almost two thousand years. The Jew has a religious significance for the Christian, and, as a consequence, he is a necessary component of the Christian view of the past.

The Jew, on the other hand, does not need Christianity to give coherence to his view of the past. Because the history of Judaism takes place within the history of Western Christian civilization, Christianity will of course occupy an important part of any history of the Jews. But the Jew can write his own history from the time of ancient Israel, through the destruction of Jerusalem in A.D. 70, down into the Middle Ages and the modern history of Judaism, including the Holocaust, the founding of the State of Israel, and most recently the Six-Day War, without giving Christianity an integral role. Christianity appears as an external factor, influencing Judaism from the outside. Religiously, it is one of the aberrations from Judaism that eventually lost all connection with the mother religion. There are, for example, only a few veiled references to Christians in ancient Jewish literature; Christian writings from the same period (third to fifth centuries) are filled, literally, with thousands of references to the Jews. Christians can't seem to get the Jews off their minds.

Christians constructed a caricature of Judaism to conform to Christian beliefs. If Judaism had no right to exist, because Christianity had taken its place, Christians thought that Jews should be excluded from the privileges accorded other members of society. Through legislation, social attitudes, and outright discrimination, Christians made it impossible for Jews to exist alongside of the Christian communities. And when the Christians saw the Jews suffering at the hands of others—destruction of their city of Jerusalem, persecution at the hands of the Romans, no land to call their own—they thought these events were proof that the Jews were being punished because they had "rejected" Jesus. In a study done several years ago, two California sociologists, Charles Glock and Rodney Stark, showed that 53 per cent of the Protestants and 52 per cent of the Roman Catholics interviewed would reject outright the statement that the "reason the Jews have so much trouble is because God is punishing them for rejecting Jesus." These attitudes of Christians are not, in the words of Glock and Stark, simply "mad notions of insignificant hate merchants";[8] they are respectable and public beliefs nurtured by the Christian tradition. In schoolbooks, in sermons, in prayers and liturgies, the Christian construction of the past supports Christian attitudes toward the Jews.

## THE DIVERSITY OF CHRISTIAN MEMORIES

Even within Christianity, different historical experiences have generated different views of the same events, and the memories of these events have in turn supported different forms of piety, belief, and polity. Most Protestants, for example, saw the Reformation as a new beginning for Christianity, and a return to the original Christian faith. The reformers were thought to have turned back the tide of corruption and put an end to the dark and tyrannous age dominated by apostate popes. Roman Catholics saw the Reformation as a repudiation of the apostolic faith. Each group singled out certain events of the period as paradigmatic. Protestants singling out the posting of the 95 Theses in Wittenberg in 1517, Roman Catholics the council of bishops gathered in the north Italian town of Trent. The Council and Decrees of the Council of Trent became a charter document of modern Roman Catholicism, whereas Protestants created a new liturgical festival, Reformation Day, with appointed lessons and prayers similar to the other festival days in the liturgical calendar.

If every construction of the past is selective, shall we call in an expert witness, an historian for example, to adjudicate the matter? The historian could, no doubt, expose the extravagances of competing views of the past; he could balance the record and shed light on the differences, but we miss the significance of collective memory if we simply test its "correctness" by some allegedly objective standard. The historical memories of religious communities do not spring full-grown from the heads of historians to be funneled into the life of the community, nor do they lie fallow in dusty tomes safely tucked away in libraries of theological seminaries. Right or wrong, true or false, beautiful or ugly, which men to imitate and which to scorn, appear as "given" to members of religious communities, through legends, proverbs, paintings and sculpture, music, architecture, prayers, dogma, and the other vehicles of religious expression. A Roman Catholic would no more have turned to the writings of Martin Luther for spiritual guidance, at least in the past, than he would have gone to the works of Mao Tse-tung or Karl Marx. Nor would a pious Methodist or Baptist have dreamed of reading the papal encyclical *Mystici Corporis* for evening devotion.

The history of the Christian church, stretching over almost two thousand years, intermingled with dozens of cultures and languages, diffused over every continent, celebrated and scorned by kings and emperors, proclaimed and perverted by popes and bishops, enriched and vulgarized by peasants and workers, adorned by artists, musicians, and architects, is a rich and fertile field for the historical imagination. Every tradition within Christianity remembers the Christian past in its own unique way. Anglicans are often considered Protestants, but it is the golden age of the church fathers or the seventeenth-century Caroline divines who live in the Anglican consciousness, not Luther, or Calvin, or Zwingli. Protestants, frequently oblivious to the medieval church as though it were a bad dream, inhabit a world shaped by the thought and piety of the sixteenth century. Until recently, Roman Catholics memorized the intricacies of medieval scholasticism and were nurtured in the piety of the Counter Reformation, while their churches looked like transplants from Italian Baroque. Orthodox Christians view the Reformation as a family squabble among Western Christians and worship in a liturgical style that transports the worshiper to ancient Byzantium. Many American Protestants act as though nothing happened between the writings of the Bible and the beginning of their own denominational tradition in the United States.

Diversity is, however, not the only rule. Protestants, Orthodox, and Catholics look back on long centuries—at least the first five hundred years—as part of a common history. The differences between contemporary Christians, i.e. the divergences within the Christian past that led to the different traditions we know today, arose at a late date in the history of Christianity, and though these later experiences color each Christian group's view of the past, all Christians remember a common beginning. Because of this common history, Christians share certain attitudes toward the Christian past that the divisions of later times did not change. Chief among these is that the apostolic age is the definitive period in the history of Christianity. This attitude takes varying forms in the different traditions: true Christianity is apostolic Christianity, and every other form of Christianity or any other historical period is to be judged by the apostolic period; whatever is distinctly Christian must be found in the apostolic age; those institutions essential to Christianity, whether the papacy, the episcopacy, apostolic succession, the Eucharist, must originate in apostolic times; the Bible, as the chief document from the apostolic period, is the sole norm for Christian life and thought. By idealizing the apostolic period, i.e. a particular historical epoch in the past, Christians have prized as values tradition, antiquity, apostolicity, uniformity, and permanence, and they have spurned change, innovation, novelty, and diversity. In language and patterns of thought, if not always in practice, Christians have loved the past more than the present or the future.

Traditionally, Christians have divided the history of Christianity into two great epochs, the time of the apostles and the time of the history of the church, the latter including everything from the end of the first century to the present. Some speak of the apostolic age as *Urgeschichte* (primal history). Most academic study of the Christian tradition, even today, distinguishes New Testament history, i.e. the study of the apostolic writings, from church history, the study of the history of Christianity. By lifting the apostolic writings out of the historical continuum, Christians have set off the period of origins as an eternal moment distinct from the temporality of the later history. Men differ on how these writings are to be interpreted, but few Christians would deny that the New Testament is the standard by which every later development is to be evaluated.

Behind this historical construction lie several assumptions: 1. Christianity always remains the same. It is obvious that the church in fifth-century Constantinople, fifteenth-century Rome, or twentieth-century Bolivia is not the same as the small Jewish sect formed in Palestine shortly after the death and Resurrection of Jesus. When Christians say that Christianity never changes, they mean that there can be no addition, alteration, or innovation within the history of Christianity that is not legitimated by the apostolic witness. Innovation, or novelty, is a distinctly bad word in the Christian vocabulary. Whenever innovations did occur, Christians claimed that they were simply a more faithful and up-to-date presentation, expression, or articulation of the original faith. Different cultural forms had enveloped the Christian message, original ideas may have "developed" beyond their original expression as a seed grows into a plant and bears fruit, but the faith itself was thought to remain the same. Only the form, expression, or formulation changes and develops. Christians believe that there was an original faith given in the apostolic age and that the responsibility of later generations is to proclaim, teach, guard, and transmit this faith to later generations.

Christian attitudes toward change do not mean that Christians cannot recognize the differences that mark the history of Christianity. We no longer build Romanesque or Gothic churches, as Christians once did; many American Protestants can recall a time when dancing, card playing, and attendance at movies or the theater were considered sinful; today these same people have no qualms about these practices. As a rule, Christians are willing to recognize change in certain areas but deny it in others. Where they hold the line, and where they waver, depend a great deal on their place within the Christian experience. Many Protestants freely grant that forms of ministry have changed, that the church was not always ruled by popes and bishops, and that these institutions do not have the sanction of apostolic authority. Yet these same people may insist upon *Sola Scriptura,* the virgin birth, or justification by grace as "unchanging" Christian beliefs. Most Roman Catholics and Episcopalians, while admitting that justification by faith may not be the "article on which the church stands or falls," would insist that the episcopal ministry, and for Roman Catholics the papacy, is essential to true and authentic Christianity. To maintain the primacy of the apostolic faith amidst the "developments" in later times, Christians have distinguished between an "essential" Christianity and various historical forms that this original faith assumes in the course of history. The original faith does not change, but its idiom is constantly changing.

"Our concept of the Church is basically influenced by the form of the Church at any given time," writes Hans Küng. "All too easily the Church can become prisoner of the image it has made for itself at one particular period in history. . . . At the same time, there is a *constant*

*factor* [my italics] in the various changing historical images of the Church, something which survives. However
much the history of mankind, of the Church and of theology may vary, it is on this that we must concentrate.
There are fundamental elements and perspectives in the
Church which are not derived from the Church itself;
there is an 'essence' which is drawn from the permanently
decisive origins of the Church."[9]

## AN AUTHORITATIVE PAST

2. A second assumption of the Christian construction
of the apostolic age is that the past is *authoritative* and
*normative* for the present and future. Paul, Matthew, and
John are the judges of Athanasius, Augustine, Bonaven-
ture, Thomas, Calvin, and Schleiermacher. The apostolic
age is not simply the first period in the history of Christianity; it is the definitive statement of what "should" and
"ought" to be the case in every generation. When Christians wish to solve a problem, initiate a new endeavor,
reform the church, or decide a theological issue, they go
to the Christian past to learn what "should" be the Christian answer. For some, the answer is as simple as "the
Bible says"; for others, their inquiry may require sophisticated historical and theological reflection on the Christian past; for others, it may depend on canons and decrees
of councils, on confessional writings, or the writings of
the church fathers or reformers or popes. The authority
of the apostolic age is extended to certain segments of
the Christian past as faithful interpretations of the mean-

ing of the apostolic faith. The "unchanging" character of Christianity, and the authority of the apostolic age, are theological ideas, but they are also part of a Christian construction of history. Over the centuries, the Christian tradition, by a process of selectivity and interpretation, has abstracted and segregated the apostolic age and made of it an ideal expression of Christianity. Amidst the variety and diversity of the Christian past, and amidst the flux and change of the historical development of Christianity, the apostolic age stands forth as a brief moment when men were closer to the gods.

Christians are not alone in their nostalgia for origins. Religious man has a yearning to return to the origins of his being, as Mircea Eliade reminds us. As men celebrate the moments of passage, birth, adolescence, marriage, they often understand these moments as the occasion for actualizing within historical time the eternal time of the gods, the perfection of the beginning, of eternity. Though this mythical consciousness is present especially in Christian piety and worship, the Christian view of the apostolic age is a historical construction of the past, i.e., it is an interpretation of actual experience, not of the gods, but of real men and women. Christians seldom speak of returning to apostolic times; rather, they say men should be "faithful" to the traditions they have received, or that they should guard the inheritance of the fathers.

Obedience is a cardinal Christian virtue. When Paul VI, in one of his recent statements on church reform, said, "Novelty for us consists essentially in a return to genuine tradition," he meant that rebellious priests and laymen should be "obedient" to the past. The historical memory of Christians validates and legitimates present practices and beliefs by placing them within an order of reality larger than the present. Instead of saying, "We do this because it pleases us," or ". . . it is the right thing to do now," or even "because I learned it from my father," we say, "We do things this way because we have always done them this way" or "because this is the apostolic way."[10]

Apostolicity is a historical construction of the past arising out of Christian experience. If the picture of the past we have inherited is the result of experiences of Christians in former ages, our age has the right, indeed the mandate, to critically examine our view of the past in light of new experiences. Hopefully, we will be able to give as great a place to change, innovation, and diversity as Christians in the past have given to tradition, permanence, and authority.

# CHAPTER II

## *The Older the Better*

At FIRST, Christians gave little thought to their own history. The Lord would return soon, they believed, and put an end to all history. When men give up their jobs, gaze into the heavens, and look for the end of the world, they write no history. Why record the past if there will be no one to remember it? The early Christian communities, in the language of current biblical scholars, were eschatological communities, i.e., they believed that the day of the Lord, proclaimed centuries earlier by the prophets, was almost upon them, and that when it came, the wheat and chaff would be sifted, the goats and sheep divided, and the righteous rule of God extended to all men. Paul, in his earliest letters, believed that his generation would live to see the end, and even though he confessed that he did not know precisely when it would come, he was confident he knew what some of the signs would be. Most of the first Christians could remember the time when Jesus was alive. His death had thrown them into confusion, but his Resurrection they took to be a sign that the final countdown of history had begun.

". . . the truth is, Christ was raised to life—the firstfruits of the harvest of the dead. . . . As in Adam all men die, so in Christ all will be brought to life; but each in his own proper place; Christ the firstfruits, and afterwards, at his coming, those who belong to Christ. Then comes the end, when he delivers up the kingdom to God the Father, after abolishing every kind of domination, authority, and power." (I Cor. 15:20–24).

## THE NEED FOR PERSPECTIVE

The past had lost meaning. God had done marvels in ancient times, but next to the wonders of the present and the promise of the future, the glory of the past was pallid and lackluster. "The splendor that once was is now no splendor at all; it is outshone by a splendor greater still." The Spirit, promised of old, had now been poured out on mankind as a "pledge of the harvest to come."

History, the handiwork of reflective men, requires perspective, distance, and memories. These the first Christians lacked. They could hardly write history, even if they wanted to, before they had made some history. The only past they knew was Israel's past, and this they used to interpret the significance of Jesus and the new life they shared. Paul preached a Christ whose life and work were part of a scheme of redemptive history stretching back to Moses, Abraham, Isaac, and Jacob. Israel's past served to legitimate the Christian claims about Jesus, to exhort, censure, and edify the Christian communities, to illustrate a point or clinch an argument with an opponent. Nevertheless, no one in the first two generations stood back at a distance to survey his own experience or the experience of the Christian communities within a historical perspective. The past provided the context, the language, the models and images, but men's minds and hearts were set on the future.

But the Lord did not return. Those who had expected to see his coming died; hope gave way to despair, certainty to bewilderment, and enthusiasm to lethargy. The first generation of Christians was convinced it would live until the Lord returned, but the second and third generations had to modify these convictions. The present no longer brimmed with promise and, paradoxically, the future grew more remote as the church moved closer to it. Much had happened since the time of Jesus. The Christian movement had begun about A.D. 30 as a tiny sect within Judaism,· and by the end of the first century it had become an independent religious force competing with other religions and philosophies across the Greco-Roman world. Christian communities could be found in most of the larger cities of the Eastern Roman Empire and some of the provincial towns, though the number of Christians may not have exceeded a few thousand by the end of the century. Most men would not have recognized the name Christian, and if they did, they probably would have had difficulty distinguishing Christianity from other oriental or Jewish cults, much as most Americans would have difficulty distinguishing Seventh Day Adventists, Church of the Nazarene, and the Four Square Gospel Church from one another even though they are quite different religious groups.

From the Christian point of view, a great deal had happened, and the Christian mission was flourishing. Yet the really big thing had *not* happened. The day of the Lord had not come; week followed on week, year on year, and finally decade on decade—and still no end! Almost imperceptibly, Christianity was becoming part of the historical process. Like other religions, it began to shape a system of beliefs, establish patterns of organization for the communities, regularize the cultus, and fix standards of behavior. Men began to realize that the magical moment had passed, that the generation that knew the Lord was dying and that another was taking its place.

As soon as Christians could look back on a previous generation, they had the makings of a past, brief as it was. But even more importantly, they realized that if there was a time in the past, there might also be a time in the future before the return of the Lord, and that they themselves might not live to the end. In this sense, Christians had to recognize their own "historicity." The Christian movement could not be viewed solely in the light of its divine origins and the expectation of a speedy end to the world. They had to view themselves in the light of other men, other experiences, other ways of life, other beliefs. I accent this seemingly obvious fact, since it is currently fashionable to attack Luke for "historicizing" Christianity and jettisoning the eschatological outlook of an earlier generation. Luke did not create the situation he found at the close of the century. Someone had to ask the obvious question: if the church was a community gathered in expectation of the end, and the Lord had not returned, how was one to explain his commitment to what seemed to be a misplaced hope? Even if the end had not come, many men still thought Jesus had spoken the truth, that he had risen from the dead, that he was present in their midst, and that he was worthy of their trust.

### LUKE AND THE CANONS OF HISTORY

The experience of the first several Christian generations, then, preceded reflection on the events of these years. Quite simply, Christians had to explain to themselves and to others why there was now a "time" of the church between the Resurrection of Jesus and the last day. Luke, a Gentile Christian writing toward the end of the first century, wrote a Gospel in the fashion of Matthew and Mark, but he also wrote an account of the spread of Christianity since the Ascension of Jesus until the death of Paul.[1] The Acts of the Apostles records events during the first three decades of Christian history, but it reflects the point of view of a Christian living a full generation later.

Luke was not a "scientific" historian coolly plotting man's religious experience on a historical graph, just as the writers of the Gospels are not biographers in our modern sense. Luke, like other early Christian writers, was a churchman interested in presenting God's saving activity in Christ; yet he chose a literary form with no real parallel in ancient literature but with closest affinity to the historical works of Greek antiquity. Many of the characteristics of ancient historical writings are missing from his work, but his preface makes clear that he had in mind a historical model as he wrote his book. He writes as a partisan for partisan purposes; yet he makes Christianity conform to some, if not all, of the canons of history. In Luke's view, Christianity was not simply the revelation of God in Jesus, to be followed by an immediate end of the world; rather, there would be a span of years between Jesus' Resurrection and his return, and during this time there would be growth, conflict, setbacks, and expansion, and this situation would continue for some time. Luke's book has no ending; it simply concludes in midstream, as though the tale may continue indefinitely.

Scholars have long debated the differences between Luke and Paul, yet the most obvious difference between them is one of perspective. Luke writes from a distance, looking back on a former age. Acts, in the words of the great modern commentator on the book, Ernst Haenchen, "tells about the age of the apostles in order to edify the Christians and to woo the Gentiles."[2] Luke had, himself, participated in some of the events he describes, but in writing his book he momentarily stepped back to survey the early progress of Christianity: "Many writers have undertaken to draw up an account of the events that have happened among us, following the traditions handed down to us by the original eyewitnesses and servants of the Gospel. And so I in my turn, your Excellency, as one who has gone over the whole course of these events in detail, have decided to write a connected narrative for you, so as to give you authentic knowledge about the matters of which you have been informed." (Luke 1:1–4)

These words, reminiscent of the prefaces of other ancient historical works, do not mean that Luke intended to write a history in the fashion of Thucydides. Nevertheless, in comparison to every other Christian writer of his generation, he is highly self-conscious about "how" he conceives his task. Paul, for example, dashed off letters to congregations without thinking of anything except the need to deal with the immediate problem. Luke, not quite aloof, but yet somewhat distant, claimed to give his readers an ordered, systematic, and continuous account of the events that happened with the coming of Jesus.

Order and continuity do not spring from the material itself. As Luke looked back, he saw many different churches in dozens of towns, each with its own tradition; he knew of different kinds of Christian leaders and missionaries, not all representing the same attitudes toward the Christian mission; he could plainly see that Christians did not everywhere practice their religion in the same way. He even gives us an insight into what must have been the chief conflict among early missionaries, namely, whether the gospel was to be preached to Greeks as well as Jews.

FIRST OUTLINE OF
A CHRISTIAN CONSTRUCTION OF THE PAST

In seeking to bring unity and order to the heterogeneity of the first thirty years, Luke began to forge, for the first time, a Christian construction of the past. Luke chose and selected what he considered of value and significance and interpreted the material he had inherited to fit into his scheme. For example, the sermons of Peter recorded in the early chapters as well as several speeches of Paul reflect the thought of Luke even though he presents his ideas in the words of Peter and Paul. His description of the spread of Christianity gives the reader the impression that the only significant missionary activity during the first generation stemmed from Paul. We see Christianity spreading from Antioch in Syria to Asia Minor, then to Greece, and finally to Rome. We hear nothing, however, about the spread of Christianity southward, especially to Alexandria, in Egypt. Alexandria, a thriving center of diaspora Jewry and one of the largest cities in the empire, was readily accessible from Palestine. Alexandria would seem to have attracted Christian missionaries, but Luke mentions not a thing. Acts "covers only a part of the history of primitive Christianity," says Jean Daniélou; "the man who wrote it was a Greek writing for Greeks, he took little interest in the Christianity of Aramaic speaking people and he was hostile to Judaeo-Christianity."[3] Further, in the conflict between Peter and Paul, Luke clearly sides with Paul, highlighting the Gentile mission to impress on his Gentile readers that Christianity is not simply a Jewish sect. In short, Luke, by selectivity, emphasis, and interpretation, creates for us a portrait of the Christian past.

As Luke looked at the church of the present, he saw the past slipping away into oblivion. The men who knew Jesus and formed the first churches were fast dying, new leaders had arisen, and the rapid spread of Christianity made it even more difficult to insure that the traditions about Jesus would be kept intact. Luke believed that the church needed "reliable guarantees of its proclamation"[4] and that the most reliable witnesses were the eyewitnesses of the first generation of Christians. Among these eyewitnesses, Luke singles out the apostolic band as particularly reliable; they not only saw and heard the things that happened around Jesus, but after his return to the Father they received in a miraculous way the gift of the Spirit. Indeed, the apostolic band was limited to a fixed number—twelve—and when one of the twelve, namely Judas, apostatized, the group had to be replenished by the addition of another apostle, Matthias. The apostles were becoming, in the Christian consciousness, the sole trustworthy witnesses to the original form of Christian faith.

Luke does not present the apostolic age or the first Christian generation as a golden age, since he is too close to the apostles to be able to overlook the problems and shortcomings of the first churches. Nor does he draw a sharp line between the church of his time and that of the earlier period. Salvation had begun with Jesus and moved through the early period and into Luke's own time, and there is no suggestion that the church of Luke's time had departed from the purity of an earlier generation, or that the church should return to its earlier ways, or even that a decline had set in. Nevertheless, Luke punctuates each section of Acts with brief summary statements idealizing the life of the first community. "They met constantly to hear the apostles teach, and to share the common life,

to break bread, and to pray. A sense of awe was everywhere, and many marvels and signs were brought about
through the apostles. . . . With one mind they kept up
their daily attendance at the temple, and, breaking bread
in private houses, shared their meals with unaffected joy,
as they praised God and enjoyed the favour of the whole
people. And day by day the Lord added to their number
those whom he was saving." (Acts 2:42–47) A few chapters later he writes: "The whole body of believers was
united in heart and soul. Not a man of them claimed any
of his possessions as his own." (Acts 4:32) In the hands
of later writers, the first generation will become a unique
and unparalleled epoch, the springtime of the church's
history, the model for all later generations.

Luke, then, passed on to later generations the bare
outline of a construction of the past suitable to the new
situation in which Christianity had found itself. The experiences of the first generation had given way to a second
and a third generation, which could not believe that Jesus
would return at any moment. The church was no longer
a community living solely in anticipation of the end of the
world; now it was a community, immersed very much in
the course of history, a community with memories of
former days and heroic leaders, and a community that
sensed that it would continue for some time before the
day of the Lord would come. There was now a time between Jesus and the end—the time of the church. Past,
present, and future now fitted into a scheme stretching
from the beginning of the world until the day when Jesus
would return. Between these two limits, creation and end-

ing, history runs its course. First there was Israel, the patriarchs, Moses, the prophets, then Jesus, his Resurrection and Ascension, the beginning of Christianity, and now the time of the church. The future promises to continue what began after the Ascension of Jesus. As the past recedes even further into the distance, the testimony of the apostles, the words of reliable witnesses, will become the only sure link with the wonders that took place when God revealed himself in Jesus.

### THE TWO MOST CREATIVE CENTURIES

Luke had no immediate successors. Between the writing of the book of Acts and the first genuine history of Christianity, written by Eusebius in the fourth century, stretch two of the most creative centuries in the history of the church, and yet no one followed up the beginning made by Luke. Books entitled Acts of John, Acts of Peter, Acts of Thomas, Paul, and Andrew survive, but these works belong to quite a different genre.[5] These works, written for the edification, instruction, and entertainment of Christians, are popular adventure stories of the achievements of the apostles. Largely legendary, the apocryphal acts of the apostles do not make any pretense of historical accuracy. Most of the other literature from this period is concerned with the defense of Christianity before the outside world, with dogmatic and theological problems within the Christian communities, and with ongoing task of nurturing Christian congregations through preaching, instruction, or the interpretation of the Bible. Men wrote apologies, polemical treatises, sermons, catechetical and devotional works, but no histories. History plays a role in some of these works, but its place is usually secondary and peripheral. In sermons, for example, the death and Resurrection of Jesus are viewed within a historical scheme of redemption from Adam through Moses and the prophets. But these homiletic flights, combining bits and pieces from Israel's history with theological speculations, are frosting on a quite unhistorical cake.

Luke's ideas, however, were not forgotten. Men had little interest in a "connected narrative" of earlier history, but they did want to know how one decided which teachers and which churches were reliable witnesses to the Christian tradition. Growing as quickly as they did, the churches had neither the time nor the inclination to insure that the many different forms of Christianity maintained some type of unity. The best men and women of Greco-Roman society had not yet begun to join the church, and able leaders were scarce. Diversity, lack of communication between Christians of different backgrounds and customs, disagreement on strategy, differences in liturgical practice, wide discrepancy on the attitudes Christians should have to the state, as well as different experiences, from toleration in some areas to repression in others, and theological disputes—these were the marks of Christianity at this time. People from different cultural backgrounds, different walks of life, speaking and writing different languages, became Christians, and not all "converted" to Christianity for the same reasons. Some were born into a Christian family, but they were in the minority; others had

Christian friends and were impressed by the style of Christian life; some thought the Christians provided a more satisfying way of life than the other philosophical schools; some were fascinated by the Christian cult and sacraments; some discovered in Christianity a new bag of mysteries, a novel and arcane language, incantations and sacred words, and a range of religious symbols almost unparalleled in antiquity.

As a new religious movement, whose way of life was yet undefined, Christianity had no one "traditional" way of doing things—no sacred book, except for the Jewish scriptures, since the canon was not yet fully formed or accepted; no central headquarters; no clear set of beliefs; no fixed organizations. What, specifically, did commitment to Christ involve? What were the distinctive marks of the Christian life-style? What should a Christian do if appointed to a civil office or called to serve in the army? Should a Christian attend public festivals and support the official cult of the Romans? How should he behave in the baths or at banquets? Was Jesus another Heracles, did he heal like Asclepius, or was he a latter-day Orpheus who died violently because he lived a pious life? Was Jesus a new Socrates? Are the stories of the Bible to be taken literally, or are they simply another form of mythology similar to the Greek myths? Will there be a resurrection of the *flesh,* or does the resurrection refer to the new life here and now through baptism? Which books are acceptable reading for Christians? Christians had always had differences, but the extremes during this period had become acute, since there was no traditional answer to most of these questions, no "party line."

How were these differences to be resolved? Everyone who claimed the name Christian could also claim that he had a right to decide what "should" be the Christian answer to these questions. Obviously, however, there had to be some public and accepted way of answering these questions for all, or at least most, Christians.

Since earliest times, Christians had appealed to tradition in settling disputes or legitimating their practices.[6] Paul exhorted the Corinthians to keep faith with the "tradition" he received "from the Lord." "For I received from the Lord what I also delivered to you, that the Lord Jesus on the night when he was betrayed took bread, . . ." (I Cor. 11:23). Behind this appeal stood the conviction that Christian truth was rooted in Jesus and that its verification ultimately had to go back to him. At first, Christians tended to rely on the words of Jesus as the test for Christian teaching and practice, but as time went on, his words, always enigmatic, became even more ambiguous and too equivocal to meet the demands of later times or to satisfy the more literal-minded bishops and teachers. The apostles seemed to speak clearly, precisely, and authoritatively, and they wrote such a great deal more than Jesus said and on topics more closely related to the new situation. The solution: let the apostles be the link between Jesus and the later church; let their testimony be the only true witness to Jesus; and let them all speak in concert, with one mind and voice. The apostles received the gospel from Jesus, who was sent from God. After receiving the faith, they

went out into the world to proclaim this message and to
found churches of their converts.

The church, wrote a bishop in Gaul, "though dispersed
throughout the whole world . . . , received from the
apostles and their disciples the faith in one God . . .
and in one Christ Jesus . . . and in the Holy Spirit. . . ."
Now that she has received this faith, she "keeps it carefully . . . and she believes these teachings as though she
had one soul and one heart, and preaches and teaches
them, and hands them down, as if she had one mouth.
For although there are different languages in the world,
the force of the tradition is one and the same. The
churches planted in Germany neither believe nor hand
down anything different; nor do those in Spain or among
the Celts or in the East or Egypt or Libya, nor those
established in the middle of the world."[7] How, then, does
one decide disputed matters among Christians? Go to
the apostolic tradition as it has been handed on in the
churches.


HEGESIPPUS' RECOLLECTIONS

We are fortunate in possessing a few fragments of a
work written during this period purporting to give a historical presentation of aspects of the Christian past. A
man named Hegesippus, something of an enigma to later
generations, wrote a book of recollections in the latter
half of the second century.[8] A Hebrew by birth, according
to Eusebius, Hegesippus became a Christian and then
made a tour of the major Christian centers of his day,

eventually journeying to Rome. His avowed purpose was to compile a list of bishops in the churches from the beginnings until his own day. These travels yielded the *Five Memoirs of Ecclesiastical Affairs,* a formless collection of reminiscences, random observations, traditions collected in his journeys, and other bits of curious information. If we had the whole of Hegesippus' work, it would probably look more like a personal diary interleaved with historical illustrations than a history. Nevertheless, his work is typical of the thinking of the time, and it had enormous significance on the writing of church history in later generations, especially on the work of Eusebius.

Hegesippus had a great interest in lists of bishops of the chief cities of the Roman Empire. Every Christian presumably had access to the apostolic writings, and yet they could not agree on how they were to be understood. If the whole church believed that apostolic tradition was the authority in the church, the question still remained: Who has transmitted this tradition faithfully? Tertullian once remarked, "Arguments about Scripture achieve nothing but a stomach-ache or a headache,"[9] for on the basis of the Bible everyone can have his way. Instead of asking simply, "What is the truth?" or "Who teaches the truth?" Christians began to ask, "Who preserved intact the apostolic tradition?" Anyone who wishes to find the truth, wrote Irenaeus, can "look at the tradition of the apostles manifested throughout the world. And we can enumerate those who were appointed bishops in the churches by the apostles and their successors [sic] up to our own day."[10] Out of this conviction grew an interest in obtaining accurate lists of the bishops who had ruled the various churches since the time of the apostles.

When I was in Corinth, says Hegesippus, "I stayed with Christians who 'continued in the true doctrine,' and together we were refreshed by this doctrine. Later I traveled on to Rome, and there I made myself a succession list as far as Anicetus. . . . And in every succession and in every city that which the law and the prophets and the Lord preach is faithfully followed."

Hegesippus' historical interest in lists of bishops is prompted by his concern for the unerring apostolic doctrine. He wrote his memoirs to defend orthodoxy as it was understood by him in mid-second century. To do this, he presents the apostles and their successors as the bearers of the true Christian faith, and he caricatures his opponents as innovators and freethinkers who have no right to the Christian inheritance.

### THE CHURCH AS A VIRGIN

The beguiling metaphor of the church as a maiden or virgin expresses precisely what he wished. They "used to call the church a virgin; for she had not yet been corrupted by vain teachings," but with the coming of false teachers, the pure and maiden church lost her virginity. Hegesippus' metaphor, in the fashion of our current cosmetic advertisements, presents the history of the church in terms of "before" and "after." The only difference is that the order is reversed, for what was "before," namely virginity, is better than what is "after." The church was a virgin because it had *not yet* been corrupted, but after a short time men such as Simon, Cleobius, Dositheus, Gorthaeus—largely unknown to us—"introduced by themselves and each in different ways their own peculiar opinions." These innovations engendered "false Christs, false prophets, false apostles, who divided the unity of the church by injurious words against God and against his Christ."[11]

We miss the force of Hegesippus' metaphor of the church as a maiden if we do not see virginity as a historical category. Hegesippus does not have in mind an ideal church abstracted from history or a religious model derived from Christian principles; he has in mind a particular historical epoch when the church was pure, unmolested, and perfect. There was a time *once* in the Christian past, at the beginning, when the church was perfect. What brought the change? Who ravished the virgin? Evil men introduced their own opinions, played with novelties, and added to the original faith. The somewhat idealized portrait of Acts here gives way to a unique and unrepeatable historical period against which all later periods will be judged. After all, a girl can be a virgin only *until* she has sexual intercourse; she can never become a virgin again.

The pattern of thinking represented here by Hegesippus was characteristic of most of the ecclesiastical writers of the period. Its chief marks are the following: 1. The apostolic age is wholly unique. It is not simply the first period in the history of Christianity, but the foundation of all later history and the standard by which all other ages are judged. 2. From this it follows that what is older in the tradition is generally thought to be closer to the apostolic age and therefore closer to the truth. 3. Uniformity is preferred to diversity, since the apostles handed on one system of truth. 4. The only sure access to this apostolic tradition is the succession of right-thinking bishops who handed on the apostolic tradition from generation to generation until it reached the present. 5. The responsibility of later generations is to preserve, guard, and keep the ancient tradition, not to introduce new ideas, add to the tradition, or alter it in any way.

### TERTULLIAN AGAINST HERESY

Tertullian, a fiery and tempestuous Latin Christian writer born about A.D. 160 in North Africa, wrote a little treatise against heresy. His purpose was to provide a definite refutation of all heresy, not just particular aberrations. Always intolerant of his opponents, Tertullian in his work surpasses himself in wit, sarcasm, and acerbity, but his very exaggerations place in bold relief the developing historical construction of Christianity.

Tertullian has not the least interest in a history of the early church; but the language he employs as well as the ideas he presents have the effect of creating a historical as well as theological picture of the first two centuries of Christianity. When Christ came to earth, he "laid down one definite system of truth," writes Tertullian, and this we "must believe without qualification." This one system of truth was transmitted through "one single tradition," which can be found in apostolic churches such as Ephesus or Rome. Jesus did not instruct his followers to go out in quest of the truth, cultivating itchy ears for other teachings; men should seek the truth *until* they find it, but when they find the truth they should, like the woman who lost and then found one of her ten pieces of silver, stop seeking. When you have found, "you have simply to *keep* what you have come to believe, for there is "nothing else to seek. . . ." We must ask of any doctrine, he continues, inclûding our own, whether "it originates in the tradition of the apostles." Let the heretics "exhibit the origins of their churches, let them unroll the list of their bishops, coming down from the beginning by succession in such a way that their first bishop had for his originator and predecessor one of the apostles or apostolic men. . . ."[12]

### THE TIME OF THE GODS

Religious man, as we observed in the first chapter, often sacralizes an original time. In the restlessness of his soul, man desires to be closer to the gods, to return to the time of origins, and regain for himself the purity, freshness, and strength of a better time. The time of the gods stands outside of historical time. Through rites and festivals, this original and primal time, mythical time, can be actualized and made present within the framework of ordinary historical time. Sacred time is repeatable and recoverable.

There are obvious parallels between this religious attitude and the historical construction of the apostolic age as a unique and ideal time period. The desire to live closer to the gods, or at least closer to the original revelation of the gods, also lives within the Christian breast. However, there is one noteworthy difference: The apostolic age is a historical epoch within ordinary time and bounded on each end by concrete historical events. In the liturgy, Christians say that they "re-present" and "make present" the life, death, and Resurrection of Jesus, and classical Christian doctrine of the Eucharist believes that the saving events of the life of Jesus are actualized within the life of the community through consecrated bread and wine. Even here, where the idea of re-presentation of sacred events is more clearly expressed, the reference is to actual historical events. But Christians have never spoken about the apostolic age the way they speak about the death and Resurrection of Jesus. They have had the good sense to recognize that the apostolic age was *another age,* another epoch, another time. Men who lived in the second, seventh, or eighteenth century felt that they were separated from the apostolic period by generations or centuries. The very way Christians constructed their history, an original period followed by a continuous succession, assumed that there is no direct access to the apostolic age. Apostolicity is a historical construction of past events.

TRUTH OLDER THAN ERROR

The Christian attraction for antiquity arises out of a

highly traditional idea of truth. Truth, according to this theory, is always older than error, and if one can go back to earliest times, he is more likely to discover truth than in recent times. What is older is better; "the real thing always exists before the representation of it; the copy comes later," writes Tertullian.[13] Translated into historical terms, this is taken by Tertullian to mean that "truth comes first and falsification afterwards." First the Lord sowed good wheat seed, and later the devil adulterated the crop. "Where was Marcion" in apostolic times? asks Tertullian. "Where was Valentinus the disciple of Plato? It is well known that they lived not so long ago, about the time of the reign of Antoninus, and at first accepted the doctrine of the catholic church at Rome under Bishop Eleutherus of blessed memory."[14] By definition, any innovation is false, for if someone introduces anything on his own authority his teaching is unapostolic, i.e. false. "Our teaching is not later: it is earlier than them all. In this lies the evidence of its truth."[15]

The appeal to antiquity and tradition was not, in the Greco-Roman world, unique to Christianity.[16] Men breathed the air of traditionalism wherever they turned— in politics, in religion, in law, in morality, from the inscriptions carved on public buildings and monuments, in the ideals for which they strove, as well as the way they viewed the ills of society. The heroic deeds of the ancestors were thought to far surpass and excel anything men did in the present. Men could not make their way in public life without the pedigree provided by a noble family. The *novus homo* always had a hard time of it. Even those who presented programs for reform or renewal presented them as the restoration of the old. Only men who were disgruntled and dissatisfied longed for change, wrote the poet Lucretius. "What could tempt those who had been at peace so long to change their old life for a new? The revolutionary is one who is dissatisfied with the old order. But one who has known no trouble in the past, but spent his days joyfully—what could prick such a being with the itch for novelty?"[17] The Romans were profoundly satisfied with their past, they gave thanks to the gods for their bounty, and they considered change and novelty strange, even sinister.

Tradition, custom, convention dominate a society that reverences the past. The good that men do, they see as a reflection of the works of their ancestors, and evil they see as a departure from the ways of the fathers. Critics of society saw Rome's greatness and good fortune as signs that Rome had remained faithful to the ancient traditions, whereas the ills of society, they considered to be signs that many had deserted the customs and traditions that had nurtured Roman piety for centuries. "The preservation of the rites of the family and of our ancestors means preserving the religious rites which, we can almost say, were handed down to us by the gods themselves, since ancient times were closest to the gods."[18] Cicero, writing in the *Laws,* a work based on customs and precedent, reflects here, in terms of Roman religion, what most ancient men felt about antiquity. Once men were closer to the gods than they are now, and the further one is from the time of the ancients the more impoverished one's mind and spirit. "The ancients are better than we," wrote Plato, "for they dwelled nearer to the gods."[19] Tradition, therefore, needed no justification; it authenticated itself simply by being old. Antiquity itself was a sign of truth, for what is older is better.

The Christian construction of the past was taking shape in a world that prized antiquity, cherished tradition, and revered men of old. Christianity was a newcomer and could make no claim on antiquity. In the defense before the Greco-Roman world, Christian apologists, following a pattern set by Jewish apologists, tried to show that Christian truth was actually similar to the teachings of the philosophers and poets, and that Plato derived much of his doctrine from Moses. In conflicts between Christians, this argument had little cash value, because most Christians assumed the authority of the apostles, but the reverence for the past created a spiritual and intellectual milieu for the understanding of the primacy of the apostolic age. If historical priority is a mark of truth, it follows that the earliest Christians had a premium on truth unmatched by any later generation.

In the space of two hundred years, Christian attitudes toward past and future had shifted dramatically. In the first century, Christians gave little thought to the past and dreamed of the future that was soon to break in upon them; by the end of the second century, their gaze had turned backward. Two hundred years is a long time— as long in ancient times as it is in the modern world. Some would say it was much longer. If the past held little meaning for the first Christians, there is no reason to think that it should have no meaning for later generations. Later generations had the privilege of looking back and identifying themselves with those who had gone before. They learned to live with the past and to love the past.

The past is never neutral, partly because it keeps enlarging before our very eyes, and partly because those who look back on the past keep changing. To serve the needs of their age, Christians in the second and third centuries constructed a historical portrait of Christianity whose outstanding characteristics were antiquity, tradition, continuity, and unity. In their construction, they shunned change and innovation, diversity and discontinuity, but they did so for good reasons. Indeed, in the language of one of the current cultural fads, Christian thinkers of this age were supremely relevant to their times. They were also extraordinarily successful. We should not blame them for that.

## CHAPTER III

# The Bishop's Maiden: History Without History

LUKE and Hegesippus were the only church historians of the first three centuries, and they were not really historians. The rightful "father of church history" is Eusebius, who lived in the fourth century. Thucydides wrote a history of the Peloponnesian War, a conflict he witnessed during his lifetime; Tacitus wrote a history of Rome in the century immediately prior to his own day; but three centuries elapsed before a genuine history of Christianity was projected.

The delay is not surprising, when one considers that in antiquity men wrote histories of peoples, of nations, of empires, but not of religions, and that the glorious deeds of ancient history—kings victorious in war, statesmen triumphant in politics—hardly suited the small religious sect that began in Palestine. By the historical standards of antiquity, Christians had produced little in the first century —one or two charismatic leaders, a few literary works of graceless prose and doubtful distinction, a few thousand people gathered in conventicles in the larger cities of the empire. There were no glorious deeds. By the end of the third century, however, *gloria* abounded. Christians could look back on brave martyrs, courageous bishops, brilliant teachers, sophisticated literary works of charm and elegance, controversies and conflicts, legends and romances and adventure stories. All that was needed was the vision, imagination, and order a historian could give to the story.

## EUSEBIUS

Eusebius was the man. His *Ecclesiastical History* is the most important historical work ever written on Christianity and one of the three or four most important books to survive from the early church. In antiquity, the book was so spectacularly successful that no one dreamed of superseding it or replacing it with another. In the period following Eusebius, three historians—two lawyers, Socrates and Sozomen, and a bishop, Theodoret of Cyrus—competed with each other over the same ground, i.e. the years from Nicaea (A.D. 325) to the middle of the fifth century. All three adopt not only the style and method of Eusebius, but they also begin their accounts where Eusebius left off, apparently satisfied that the first period needed no redoing. Read and reread, the *Ecclesiastical History* became the model for all later writing of church history. As one nineteenth-century editor put it, "With the Bible in the right hand and Eusebius' *Ecclesiastical History* in the left hand, we can take on all the enemies of Christ's church." Many Christians have done just that.

Eusebius was born in the latter half of the third century in Palestine, where he spent most of his life. We know nothing of his family and early years. During his student days, he met a certain Pamphilius, who introduced him to the study of history, and later provided the books, money, and encouragement for Eusebius to pursue his own research. Pamphilius, a native of Phoenicia and a priest in the church, was one of those charming patrons so dear to scholars, a man both zealous for learning and rich. Over the years, he had collected a remarkable library of Christian and non-Christian manuscripts. In the congenial setting offered by Pamphilius' library, Eusebius indulged his appetite for Christian antiquities, and began the task of collecting and organizing materials for the history. The task was enormous, chiefly because no one had prepared the way for him and because Christianity already had three hundred years of history behind it. The apostolic age was further distant from Eusebius than the framers of the Constitution are distant from us!

The late third century, a time of growing uncertainty and confusion in the Roman Empire, was for the Christian church a time of increasing self-confidence, even optimism, marked by brief moments of doubt and fear. The Christians had begun to sense that the future lay with them, ·but the recurrence from time to time of persecution and repression cast a shadow over their rising hopes. Good fortune accompanied Eusebius' early life, for he was born shortly after the great persecution under the emperor Decius in 250. He had, no doubt, heard stories about the evil emperor and valiant martyrs, but these tales, edifying though they were for Christian piety, seemed like a thing of the past. Eusebius grew to maturity during the long years of peace and tranquillity between 260 and 300. Not until he was over forty years old did he see for himself that the Roman state and the Christian religion were not yet happy and contented bedfellows. Suddenly, in 303, the long peace ended: churches were razed, the Scriptures put to the flames, bishops taken into prison and exiled, and Eusebius' patron and friend Pamphilius imprisoned and later beheaded. Persecution shattered hopes and aspirations. In a flash, Christians realized that their impressive growth in numbers, prestige, and influence during the past century did not insure immunity from the capricious power of the emperors.

The trauma of these years never left Eusebius. His history would reflect the shape of his own life—trust in good emperors and extravagant praise for the benevolence of Roman rulers, alternating with acrimony and bitterness at the foes of the church. Eusebius survived the persecutions, but he never forgot the horror of those days nor the elation he experienced at the new age inaugurated by Constantine. Singing the praises of his new ruler as loudly as he denounced Constantine's evil predecessors, Eusebius wrote, "From that time on a day bright and radiant, with no cloud overshadowing it, shone down with shafts of heavenly light on the churches of Christ throughout the whole world. . . . Thus all men living were free from oppression by the tyrants. . . . Above all, for us who had fixed our hopes on the Christ of God there was unspeakable happiness, and a divine joy

blossomed in all hearts. . . . Emperors . . . , by a succession of ordinances in favor of the Christians, confirmed
still further and more surely the blessings that God show-
ered upon us; and a stream of personal letters from the
emperors reached the bishops, accompanied by honors
and gifts of money[!]. . . ."[1] The joy of freedom and
peace banished all fear of former terror.

Eusebius had been ordained before the persecutions.
Shortly after the peace of the church, the citizens of
Caesarea elected him bishop. As the ranking prelate in
the area, he was invited in A.D. 315 to Tyre, a town in
Palestine on the Mediterranean coast, to deliver the address at the dedication of a sparkling new basilica. His
theme was exultation and jubilation over this glorious
building—a symbol of the victory of the church. A few
years later, he attended the council of Nicaea, where he
delivered the opening address, and not insignificantly,
took his seat in a place of honor next to the emperor.
Again he intoned a song of praise. From the time of the
council of Nicaea in A.D. 325 until the death of Constantine in 337, Eusebius commuted back and forth between
his home church and the imperial court. When absent
from Constantinople, the bishop corresponded regularly
with the emperor; when they were together, the emperor recounted to the bishop the tales of his adventurous
life. Eusebius took careful notes, anticipating the publication of his *Life of Constantine.* An urbane and cultivated
man, Eusebius thrived on the extravagances of the Byzantine court. He is reported to have been so much a part
of the imperial family that on one occasion he rebuked

and then catalogued. There were no indexes of early Christian literature!

History does not write itself; after the work of reading and gathering information, the historian must weed out, select, and eventually order the material according to a pattern. As Eusebius looked back over the first three hundred years of Christianity, he observed, by his own admission, a lovely pasture filled with an impressive variety of flowers. As he walked through the meadow, he picked those flowers that seemed "relevant to the task [he had] undertaken," and these he put together within a "continuous narrative."

The period Eusebius surveyed included the beginning and early development of almost everything we associate with Christianity today: its system of belief, its primary institutions (e.g. the monarchial episcopate), the canon of the New Testament, and the Apostles' Creed. During this period, Christianity grew from a small Jewish sect to become the major religion of the Roman world; it had suffered persecution at the hands of Roman emperors, but it had also lived through long years of peace. Many Christian authors had the leisure to write dozens of books; a distinctive Christian language grew up on the basis of the Greek and Latin of classical times. People from every walk of life, in all classes and with different means, men and women of great erudition and sophistication, as well as farmers, merchants, artisans, and soldiers now made up the Christian populace. Which of these flowers were "relevant" to the task Eusebius set before himself? How was he to give order to his history?

In his apology to the Greeks and Romans, the *Praeparatio Evangelica,* Eusebius cited the familiar charge against the Christians that they were a new and strange innovation. Quoting from Porphyry's work *Against the Christians,* he writes that Christians practiced a "new and strange" life whose only fruit was "impiety and atheism." The Christians, said Porphyry, have "turned away from those recognized as gods by all Greeks and Barbarians, in cities and in the country, with every type of sacrifice, mysteries, initiations, by kings and lawgivers and philosophers, and have chosen what is impious and atheistic among men." The same charge against Christians appears in the opening chapters of the *Ecclesiastical History.* We must answer those, writes Eusebius, who think of "our Savior and Lord, Jesus Christ, as a newcomer, because of the date of his sojourn in the flesh. But to prevent anyone from imagining that his teaching either [sic] was new and strange, as being put together by a man of recent date no different from his fellows, let us now deal briefly with this point." To the tradition-oriented society of the Roman Empire, the Christian movement appeared as a new invention, started "only yesterday," whose way of life led men away from the "customs of the fathers."[3]

Eusebius conceived of his *Ecclesiastical History* as an apology for the truth of Christianity, but instead of following the older pattern of apologetics practiced by Christians for centuries and by Eusebius himself in his *Praeparatio Evangelica,* he charted a new course. Old-style Christian apologetics defended Christianity against its critics by reasoned arguments; Eusebius presents a sys-

tematic and continuous account of Christianity since its
origins. But why? Three hundred years would hardly impress the Romans of the great antiquity of the Christians.
Eusebius admits that the Christians are a "new people"
and a new name, but they can trace their history back
through the Jews to creation itself. Even though the revelation in Christ took place relatively late in human history, Christ himself exists eternally, and the Christian
religion is "none other than the first, most ancient, and
most original of all religions, discovered by Abraham and
his followers, God's beloved." The new name, the new
way of life, and the new teaching are deceptive, for what
Christians teach and the way they live are not recent "in-
ventions" but the "natural concepts of those whom God
loved in the distant past."[4]

### DIVINE ORIGINS

Book I of the *Ecclesiastical History* includes a minor
theological treatise on the divinity of Christ. In this section, Eusebius tries to establish that the origins of the
church are divine because the church has its beginnings
in the dispensation given by the divine Christ. "My book
will start with a conception too sublime and overwhelm-
ing for man to grasp—the dispensation and divinity of
our Savior Christ. Any man who intends to commit to
writing the record of the church's history is bound to go
right back to Christ himself, whose name we are privileged
to share, and to start with the beginning of a dispensation
more divine than the world realizes."[5]

What the world did not realize, according to Eusebius, or at least acknowledge, was that Christ was not a new-comer simply because he had appeared only recently; Christ revealed himself to the apostles at a late moment in history, but the revelation he gave them is not a new teaching, but the first and most ancient faith. In the history of the Christian church, in so far as it is founded on the teaching of the apostles, men see the divine truth as it exists in time.

The first and most important "flower" in church history, then, is the succession of bishops, because bishops are the only sure link between later Christian generations and the apostolic age.

"The chief matters to be dealt with in this work," writes Eusebius, "are the following.

"1. The lines of succession from the holy apostles, and the periods that have elapsed from our Savior's time to our own; the many important events recorded in the story of the Church; the outstanding leaders and heroes of that story in the most famous Christian communities; the men of each generation who by preaching or writings were ambassadors of the divine word.

"2. The names and dates of those who through a passion for innovation have wandered as far as possible from the truth, proclaiming themselves the fonts of knowledge falsely so called while mercilessly, like savage wolves, making havoc of Christ's flock.

"3. The calamities that immediately after their conspiracy against our Savior overwhelmed the entire Jewish race.

"4. The widespread, bitter, and recurrent campaigns

launched by unbelievers against the divine message, and the heroism with which when occasion demanded men faced torture and death to maintain the fight in its defense.

"5. The martyrdoms of later days down to my own time, and at the end of it all the kind and gracious deliverance accorded by our Savior."[6]

This listing of topics, placed at the very beginning of the *Ecclesiastical History*, fairly bristles with polemics. Eusebius intends to present a history of the divine truth as it met resistance, conflict, and persecution by its foes. Bishops in apostolic succession, Christian teachers and leaders, and martyrs will be witnesses to this truth, whereas heretics, evil emperors, and Jews will conspire against the Faith. His answer, then, to the critics of Christianity is twofold. On the one hand, he tries to show that Christianity is not a recent invention, but the eternal truth as it now appears among men. The apparent novelty of Christianity is deceptive; actually, it is the oldest and truest religion, and the inability of its detractors to recognize this is not a judgment against Christianity, but a condemnation of the church's foes, because they themselves have departed from the eternal truth. Emperors only reveal their own "impiety" when they persecute the Christians in the name of piety. Secondly, the true innovators are not the Christians, but the heretics, who have strayed from the truth. Eusebius calls the Montanists "newfangled," Paul of Samosata an "innovator," and the heresy of Artemon a "recent novelty, since they who introduced it wished to clothe it with the grave garb of antiquity."[7]

Historical writing, if it is not to be more than a retelling
of tales and legends of the past, must not only be selective, but critical. Every historian uses, sometimes con-
sciously but frequently unconsciously, certain critical
principles to interpret and evaluate his sources, but also
to judge men and events. We expect that a historical account of the term of a president or a prime minister will
compare and contrast his accomplishments with those of
his predecessors and successors, that his handling of domestic affairs or internal problems will be viewed in light
of its success or failure, and that the men he chooses to
serve as secretary of state, attorney general, or defense
secretary are indicators of the man's stature. Eusebius,
too, had a critical principle. It was not, however, derived
from a comparison of Christianity to Mithraism, or by
contrasting the administrative accomplishments of bishops
as opposed to Roman governors, or even by showing
how Christianity had improved the lot of man. Eusebius'
critical principle comes from a theological idea of the
truth of Christianity and the church.

How could it be otherwise? After three centuries of
competing with other religions and philosophies, and long
years of conflict with emperors and provincial governors,
Christianity had reached the pinnacle of power. It had
not yet, it is true, become the official religion of the Roman
world—this would take place two generations later—but it
had won not simply a place in the sun, but a seat in the
imperial palace. Intelligent critics of Christianity were disappearing; many Christians could believe that the case
for Christianity against paganism was almost won. A few

details had to be taken care of, but in the main the case was closed. The Scriptures had sustained the attack, the new way of life clearly won more converts than any rival, Christian teaching had stood the test of time, and the church had endured. Why compare Christianity to Mithraism or the teaching of Jesus to that of Plato, Aristotle, or the Stoics? Christian apologists had been doing that for several centuries. Christianity was not another religion among religions. Clearly it was the only true religion given by God. Men do not embrace a new religion by the thousands, change their lives, turn from evil to good, the apologists argued, if a religion does not come from God. To a fourth-century Christian, and especially one with the experience of Eusebius, the claim that Christianity was true and divine seemed self-evident. All that was needed now was a presentation of how this divine truth had fared in the course of history. Once men had judged Christianity by their standards; now Christianity was the standard. This divine truth is Eusebius' critical principle.

### THE HERETICS

He exercises this principle chiefly on the heretics, who "through a passion for innovation have wandered as far as possible from the truth." Eusebius saw many weeds among the flowers. The Christian past was strewn with a great many heretics, who loved the truth no more than did the emperors who persecuted the faith. These false teachers, though Christians by name, are not part of the true history of Christianity, for they themselves are opponents of the very truth the church proclaims. In sifting out the men and documents of the first three centuries and separating the heretics from the orthodox, Eusebius was no trail blazer; here he had predecessors enough. As he read through the early Christian writings, he simply adopted as his own the criteria of selectivity used by earlier theologians. A list had long been in existence: Irenaeus was acceptable, Valentinus was not; Hippolytus taught apostolic doctrine, whereas Beryllus bishop of Bostra did not; Marcion was an innovator, Tertullian a faithful disciple of the apostles.[8] Eusebius' critical principle does not simply set off the church from paganism; it also discriminates between different forms of Christianity.

Heretics and evil emperors give life to Eusebius' history. Without them, the book would not only be dull; there would be no book! What would there be to tell if the apostolic faith had met no resistance? The book is a history of conflict and controversy. If there had been no resistance to the faith, the beginning of the history would be the end! As the book presently stands, the ending is a celebration of the triumph of the apostolic faith. Both persecutors and heretics have been put to rout, and if new persecutors or heretics arise, the Christian emperor will see to it that the apostolic faith is protected. Eusebius' history tells no story; it reports on an eternal conflict taking place over and over in countless different situations, in different lands, and among different peoples. His history reads like a set of one-act dramas strung together without plot, movement, or development. Eusebius adopts, for example, the reigns of Roman emperors as the external structure of his history, but they bear no relation to events within the history. Ecclesiastical events are simply slotted into the reigns of different emperors. For this reason, the divisions within the book are highly arbitrary and artificial. Some Christian authors appear under one emperor and then later under his successor, with little regard to the continuity in the man's life. The reader has no sense of the differences between the men and problems of one age and those of several generations or centuries later. Two peaks—the apostolic age on one end, and the Constantinian age on the other—dominate the horizon, with a flat plain in between.

COMPELLING LEGENDS

The Eusebian construction of the Christian past was, because of its very simplicity, extraordinarily compelling for Christians of his own time. And lest we forget, it was for fourth-century Christians that he was writing. Let the following serve as illustrations: Already legends were circulating concerning the "apostolic origin" of the Apostles' Creed, a catechetical statement of faith developed during the second century. According to popular opinion, expressed in a work written at the beginning of the fifth century, the creed had been formulated by the apostles before they set out to missionize the world.

"As they were therefore on the point of taking leave of each other, they first settled on an agreed norm for their future preaching, so that they might not find themselves, widely separated as they would be, giving out different doctrines to the people they invited to believe in Christ. So they met together in one spot and, being filled with the Holy Spirit, compiled this brief token, as I have said, of their future preaching, each making the contribution he thought fit; and they decreed that it should be handed out as standard teaching to believers."

Later tradition embellished this account by assigning one phrase of the creed to each apostle. According to an eighth-century sermon, when the apostles gathered after the Ascension, "Peter said 'I believe in God the Father almighty . . . Andrew said 'and in Jesus Christ His Son . . . James said 'Who was conceived by the Holy Spirit.' . . ."[9] These legends have no place in Eusebius' history, but the theological and historical assumptions behind these legends are the same ones that support Eusebius' construction of the Christian past.

Another example, this one illustrating the attitude of Christians at that time to doctrinal change, is the principles adopted by translators of early Christian documents. Beginning in the late fourth and early fifth centuries, Christians began, in earnest, to translate into Syriac, Latin, and other languages books that lent support to their own theological views. Sometimes the translator discovered to his chagrin that his favorite author did not express himself precisely in the thought patterns or expressions considered acceptable, i.e. apostolic, to the translator. For example, if a translator lived after the Trinitarian controversies, he would have difficulty understanding statements in earlier writers suggesting that Christ was "subordinate" to the Father. Conclusion: they must not have meant what they said, and their teaching should be expressed in a fashion consistent with the translator's teaching, since the translator believed he taught nothing other than the original apostolic faith.

Rufinus, a fourth-century Christian author, translated a number of works of Origen, the great Alexandrian theologian who lived over a century earlier. By the time Rufinus lived, many of Origen's opinions, considered acceptable in Origen's own day, had become suspect. When Rufinus came to translate Origen's book *On First Principles,* he discovered that many of Origen's statements did not harmonize with the orthodox doctrine of Rufinus' day. Rufinus says in the preface that he will follow the practice of an earlier translator who, when he found "in the original a good many statements likely to cause offense, so smoothed over and emended these in his translation that a Latin reader would find in them nothing out of harmony with our faith." In brief, the translator is not only to translate Origen's Greek into the translator's Latin, but also he is supposed· to translate Origen's ideas into the orthodoxy of the translator's age. Rufinus says that he would follow this practice to the "best of [his] ability if not with an equal degree of eloquence" as his predecessor. I will "take care," writes Rufinus "not to reproduce such passages from the books of Origen as are found to be inconsistent with and contrary to his true teaching."[10]

## THE STANDARDS OF TRUTH

Eusebius was too knowledgeable about the past and

too intelligent to believe that everything men took for granted as Christian in the fourth century originated with the apostles. Obviously, the tiny band of apostles who followed Jesus, and the churches founded by these apostles, could not simply be identified with the world-wide religious organization at the beginning of the fourth century. Changing times required new rules and regulations to govern the communities; different areas of the church practiced different liturgical customs. Easter, for example, was not celebrated everywhere on the same date. In some matters, the apostles had not given an opinion, and the churches had to decide matters for themselves.

But in the matter of prime importance, dogma, differences of opinion were strictly ruled out. There was one faith, and the dogmas of Christianity did not change with the passage of time. What Christians believed at the beginning of the fourth century was the same original faith they believed in the second century, and this in turn was simply a restatement of the apostolic faith. Eusebius said, disapprovingly, of Tatian that he was "bold enough to alter some of the apostles' expressions as though trying to rectify their phraseology." He attacks Florinus and Blastus, two heretics, because they "led many churchmen astray . . . each trying in his own way to innovate on the truth." Eusebius approves of the letter of Clement of Rome because in it he finds "apostolic teaching," but the Pseudo-Clementines he rejects because "there is no mention whatever of them by early writers, nor do they preserve in its purity the stamp of apostolic orthodoxy."[11]

Whoever crosses the pages of the *Ecclesiastical History* must conform to the same standard of truth, whether he lived in the second or third century, in Egypt or in Asia Minor or in Gaul. Eusebius portrays men, events, and ideas either as moments in the expression of the eternal truth or as a deviation from this truth.

The metaphor of virginity held the same fascination for Eusebius as it did for Hegesippus. Indeed, it was Eusebius who copied out the passage on the church as a virgin from Hegesippus' *Memoirs* and preserved it in his *Ecclesiastical History*. Hegesippus had been discussing the time when he thought new ideas were first introduced into Christianity, in the early second century. Commenting on the passage, Eusebius writes:

"Until then the church had remained a virgin, pure and uncorrupted, since those who were trying to corrupt the wholesome standard of the saving message . . . lurked somewhere under cover of darkness. But when the sacred band of the apostles had in various ways reached the end of their life, and the generation of those privileged to listen with their own ears to the divine wisdom had passed on, then godless error began to take shape through the deceit of false teachers, who now that none of the apostles was left threw off the mask and attempted to counter the preaching of the truth by knowledge falsely so called."[12]

For Eusebius, the idea of the church as a virgin is clearly a historical category referring to a *time* in the Christian past. Pure and virginal Christianity was apostolic Christianity; since the church had been ravaged by false teaching, later generations can only strive to approximate the original faith.

Ferdinand Christian Baur, the great nineteenth-century church historian, once wrote a book on Christian historiography. Over a hundred years ago, he recognized clearly that the Eusebian construction of the past, because of its preoccupation with the eternal truth of Christian dogma, was unable to make a place for change in the historical experience of Christians. Christianity began with the dogma of the divinity of Christ, and the primary interest of the historian of Christianity is to record the fortunes of this dogma in the years since it was first given to the apostles. If there is change or novelty, it must either result from heresy or occur in peripheral and non-essential areas —never in dogma. "While dogma [in Eusebius' view] remains always the same and represents in its whole temporal manifestation only the pure apostolic tradition, the heresies form a self-composed sequence of continually changing phenomena, which in their continual reaction to dogma only serve to place the eternal, unshakable truth of the latter in a vivid light."[13]

I am reminded of a story told me recently of a mother who returned to her daughter's college for an alumnae meeting. Parents and faculty were vigorously debating the direction of the college's future—parents demanding that things remain the way they remembered them, and the faculty arguing that changes were inevitable. At one point, an especially vociferous mother got up and shouted, "I want my daughter to remain just what she is now and to get from college just what I got when I went here. I don't want her to change."

### HISTORY WITHOUT CHANGE

The bishop loved the church—as a maiden! He wanted her to remain pure, untouched, virginal. But how can virginity change without losing its purity? Can virginity become more virginal? Only one path leads away from perfection—the road to imperfection. Any historical development, any innovation, addition, or alteration away from the apostolic faith can only be a deviation. Eusebius wrote a history of Christianity in which there is no *real history*, for there is no place for change in his portrait of Christianity. The true church always remains the same from generation to generation, and the events that do in fact constitute the historical experience of Christianity are either the false innovations of heretics and the persecutions of evil emperors, or the efforts of faithful Christians to withstand persecution and defend the true faith against error. There is no genuine history, for there *can be* no history; Christianity is and remains forever what it was at its beginning. In Eusebius' history, nothing really happens —or, more accurately, nothing *new* happens. The history of the church is a history of an eternal conflict between the truth of God and its opponents.

For three hundred years, Christians had been sorting out and interpreting their experiences. A distinctive Christian construction of the past emerged during these years, but it had not yet taken shape in a historical narrative.

Eusebius seized on the glorious moment provided by the peace of the church to gather the strands of earlier tradition and to weave them into a symmetrical pattern. As we observed in the first chapter, every historical construction of the past selects what it considers important and idealizes those moments that seem particularly expressive of the community's self-understanding. Eusebius narrowed the vision of the Christian past by constructing a historical memory that made apostolic doctrine the center of ecclesiastical history. But he gave to the Christians of his day a vision of the past attuned to the traditions they had received from earlier Christians, and more importantly, a vision attuned to the spirit of the age. Eusebius wished to write, in a new fashion, an apology for Christianity, and his apology, because it was written just as victory was within grasp, breathed no longer the spirit of a persecuted minority, but the mood of triumph and exaltation.

In the end, Eusebius' history is uncritical. Like other historians, he evaluates the men he portrays, but he is unable to bring any critical standard to bear on the church itself, the rightful subject matter of his history. The patrimony of Eusebius is a theological conception of church history formed by a theological idea of Christian truth. History in the Eusebian model will always be history from within, history by Christians about Christianity, history from the perspective of Christian faith. The true church is always true; faithful bishops are always faithful; heretics are always thought to be innovators; and persecuting emperors always persecute the church to serve their evil ends. Only deviants introduce new ideas, sow seeds of falsehood, or create division. The enemy is always outside, and even when he is found inside the church, Eusebius is confident he can trace the origins to outside sources. Only good men rule the church; bishops never confuse orthodoxy and personal ambition; martyrs are never overzealous fanatics. Eusebius and his disciples cannot contemplate the possible limitations and faults of the Christian movement, to say nothing of the demise of Christianity.

Erik Erikson, the Harvard psychoanalyst and now historian, tells in his recent book on Mahatma Gandhi how the remembrance of past events is colored by the *time* in a person's life when they are remembered.

"If history," he writes, "is a collection of events which come to life for us because of what some actors did, some recorders recorded, and some reviewers decided to retell, a clinician attempting to interpret an historical event must first of all get the facts straight. But he must apply to this task what he has learned, namely to see in all factuality some relativities which arise from the actors', the recorders' and the reviewers' motivations. . . . The psycho-historian will want to inquire in some detail after the stage of life in which the actor acted, the recorder recorded, and the reviewer reviewed. He will want to learn about the place of that stage in the life cycle of each of these individuals; and he will want to relate their life cycles to the history of the communities."[14]

The same events, remembered in youth, in middle age, or in old age, will look quite different. What Erikson says here about individuals is also the case for historical communities. The memory of events in one stage of the church's history may differ sharply from its memory at a later stage, and the norms of selectivity exercised at one period may be quite inapplicable at a later stage.

The first history of Christianity was written when the history of the Roman Empire and the history of the Christian church were converging into one universal Christian history. Once Christians and Romans had contested with each other over the true form of piety toward God, but now they joined hands to honor the one true God—Father, Son, and Holy Spirit. "Men had now lost all fear of their former oppressors," wrote Eusebius; "day after day they kept dazzling festival; light was everywhere, and men who once dared not look up greeted each other with smiling faces and shining eyes. They danced and sang in city and country alike, giving honor first of all to God our sovereign Lord . . . and then to the pious emperor with his sons, so dear to God." The world had been "wiped clean of the hatred of God. . . ."[15] The first history of Christianity was written at a time of elation and victory. The apostolic faith, the novelty of three hundred years earlier, had shown itself to be the original and oldest religion given by the gods at the springtime of human history.

## CHAPTER IV

# *No Faith Except the Old*

I⊤ was fall A.D. 448. For weeks, bishops had been streaming into Constantinople, the eastern capital of the Roman Empire. They came from all over northwestern Asia Minor, from Chalcedon, Nicomedia, Basilinopolis, Apamea, Nicaea, Candra, to a local council called to hear the case of Eutyches, the head of a monastery in the vicinity. Eutyches, an elderly monk, pious but somewhat dull-witted, had committed the unfortunate error of expressing himself carelessly and imprecisely on the nature of the person of Christ. For several generations, Christian thinkers had been concerned with defining the relation between the divine and human in Christ. Was he a divine being who had assumed human flesh, but had not taken on a human psyche, i.e. the consciousness of an actual historical person? Or did his human consciousness exist alongside of his divine consciousness as the son of God? If neither of these, how did the human and divine relate to each other in Christ? A definitive answer was not yet forthcoming, but Eutyches' statements were ambiguous enough to cause some bishops to question his orthodoxy. He seemed to make the divine element in Christ so predominant that there was little place for his human nature. By merging the human nature into Christ's divine nature, Eutyches seemed to collapse the distinction between the divine and the human in Christ.

At the council, Eutyches' greatest support came from the bishops of Egypt and especially their outspoken patriarch Dioscorus, bishop of Alexandria. Though most of the Egyptian bishops were careful not to use the dubious language of Eutyches—they always insisted that Christ was fully divine *and* fully human—their views were quite congenial to his position. When Eutyches was called to appear before the council, he knew that he could count on the support of the Egyptians, but he also realized that he did not have enough votes to carry the full chamber of bishops. As was customary, the bishops first requested a statement of faith by the accused, but Eutyches, realizing the probable outcome, pleaded that he had other obligations to fulfill; when they requested him to appear a second time, he claimed that he was sick; and finally, after a third appeal, he hid behind his monastic vow of seclusion. Later, when he was assured of the support of the imperial chamberlain Chrysaphius, he appeared before the bishops and brought with him into the council chamber a great army of monks and other officials. His efforts to sway the council failed, however, and after hearing his confession of faith the bishops charged him with heresy.

Eutyches was craftier than the bishops realized. Upon his return to the monastery, he regrouped his forces and began the diplomatic and political maneuvers necessary to make an appeal. In less than a year he was called to ap-

pear, not before a local synod such as that in Constantinople a year earlier, but before a world-wide council con-
voked by the emperor. Again the letters went out to the
bishops, not simply in Asia Minor but to the whole church,
and again they collected their advisers and aides to journey
to an ecumenical council, this time in Ephesus. The fourth-
century Latin historian Ammianus Marcellinus quipped
that the Christians quarreled so frequently and attended so
many councils that the imperial transit system was on the
verge of breaking down. With bishops traveling to and fro
across the empire, ordinary citizens could never find car-
riages when they were needed.[1]

THE ROBBER COUNCIL

Later generations know the council in Ephesus in 449
as the Robber Council (*Latrocinium*) because Leo, the
bishop of Rome at the time and one of the losers, gave it
that name in one of his letters. He was not far from the
truth. The council was a riotous and boisterous affair, at
which the bishops debated with their fists instead of with
arguments. Business took place amidst great tumult, the
clergy accusing one another not only of heresy but of deceit and dishonesty. Eutyches was the beneficiary. After
examining his statement of faith, the bishops, now representing the whole church, accepted his appeal and reversed
the earlier decision. Eutyches was acquitted.

In his confession before the council, Eutyches told of his
zeal for orthodoxy since youth, his lifelong battle with
heretics, and his faithfulness to the apostolic faith as ex-

pressed by the bishops at Nicaea over one hundred years earlier. At one point, he cited the text of the creed of Nicaea, but his wording of the text differed from that familiar to most of the bishops. Actually, he read from an earlier version, which had since been forgotten. When he concluded his speech, a certain Eusebius—not the historian —bishop of Dorylaeum, a town in Phrygia in Asia Minor, and an ardent opponent of Eutyches, blurted out, "He is lying. . . . This is not the statement of faith." At once, Dioscorus, bishop of Alexandria, a friend of Eutyches, and the man destined to lose most if Eutyches was not acquitted, jumped to his feet. "I know four books containing this creed. Is this not what the bishops decided?"

Immediately another bishop, Diognetus, rose to speak: "Unfortunately, that which the synod of the holy fathers in Nicaea decided received *additions* from the holy fathers because of the evil opinions of Apollinaris, Valentinus, and Macedonius, and the like, and the phrase 'descended and made flesh from the Holy Spirit and the Virgin Mary' was added to the symbol of the holy fathers. This Eutyches left out since he is an Apollinarian and Apollinaris deceived the holy synod of Nicaea, accepting the text according to his own view."

At the word "additions," the Egyptian bishops, always the most zealous defenders of orthodoxy, especially when their own views were at stake, shouted, "Nothing is added and nothing is to be taken away. Let the teachings of the fathers stand. Let the decisions of the bishops of Nicaea stand. Let the things of the Holy Spirit stand. The orthodox emperor has commanded this."[2]

The Egyptians claimed to be offended by the "additions" to the Nicene Creed. The creed had been formulated at the council of Nicaea in A.D. 325, but during the course of the fourth century the phrase "descended and made flesh from the Holy Spirit and the Virgin Mary" was added to emphasize that Christ was fully human. The Egyptians knew that this particular phrase was not part of the original wording and that it had been added because some had denied Christ's full humanity, but what they did not admit was that some in their own ranks were quite uncomfortable with the implications of the additional phrase. What actually was happening at the council was that the Egyptians realized that if Eutyches' appeal was rejected and his previous condemnation sustained, the Egyptian position would, by implication, also be censured. Under the presidency of Dioscorus, the Egyptians were able to gain and keep control of the council and to counter the opposition that came from the Roman delegation. Leo, bishop of Rome, had sent his legates to the council with instructions to support a condemnation of Eutyches and a reversal of the decision of Constantinople the year before. But Leo lost this round of the controversy. Eutyches' acquittal at Ephesus in 449 was a victory for Alexandria and Egypt over Rome. The triumph was, however, short-lived.

## THE COUNCIL OF CHALCEDON

Less than a year later, the emperor, Theodosius II, who had presided over the council and who made its decisions the law of the empire, fell off his horse while on a hunting expedition and died shortly thereafter. His successor, Marcian, was immediately receptive to the appeal of Leo to convene another council. Within months, the new emperor began to arrange for yet another gathering of the bishops. This council was to be held at Chalcedon, a town a short distance from Constantinople. Only two years had passed since the last council, but once again the bishops—most of them the same men—had to journey to another ecclesiastical synod. The year was A.D. 451. By the time the bishops convened, Eutyches, whose influence, never considerable, had begun to wane, had been forgotten and they turned to bigger game—Dioscorus, the patriarch of Alexandria.

Dioscorus had made the double mistake of supporting the somewhat extreme position of Eutyches on the person of Christ *and* attempting to excommunicate the bishop of Rome. Even in the early fifth century, when Rome was still in the process of consolidating her authority, one did not with impunity excommunicate the bishop of Rome. Dioscorus, who only two years earlier had sat at the pinnacle of power, found that many of his former friends and supporters had swung to the other side. The bishops of the Eastern empire forsook Alexandria and joined with Rome to topple the proud Egyptian bishop.

Dioscorus was deposed from his office, excommunicated, and banished by imperial authorities to Gangra in Paphlagonia, a province in north-central Asia Minor. The council's theological statement, worked out by a committee in the final sessions, asserted that the true catholic faith taught that Christ was fully God and fully man.

"We confess one and the same Lord Jesus Christ and we all teach harmoniously that he is the same perfect in Godhead, the same perfect in manhood, truly God and truly man . . . acknowledged in two natures without confusion, without change, without division, without separation."

In the decree, the bishops also announced: "With a common vote we have excluded the doctrines of error and rescued the unerring faith of the fathers," and by affirming the faith of "the 150 fathers at Constantinople [A.D. 381] and the 318 holy and blessed fathers at Nicaea [A.D. 325] we have destroyed the heresies which had sprung up and we made our teaching conform to the same catholic and apostolic faith."[3]

We need not follow the melancholy course of these debates any further. Chalcedon, called to heal wounds in the church and to settle theological differences, led to even greater division, disharmony, and misunderstanding. The council of Chalcedon was the beginning, not the termination, of the controversy over the meaning of the person of Christ. Even today, fifteen centuries after the council, theologians are still pondering the meaning of its dogmatic statement and are trying to find a more satisfactory way to express the relation between the divine and human in Christ. What interests us here, however, is not the disputes over dogmatic terms nor the theological meaning of the formulations issued by the assembled clergy at Chalcedon, but *how* the bishops who gathered in council understood their assignment and how they viewed their relation to earlier Christian tradition. What do the debates over the

person of Christ in the fifth century, as well as other theological controversies in the early church, contribute to our
understanding of the Christian construction of the past?

"Nothing is added and nothing is to be taken away." This
statement expresses as well as any other the mind of the
bishops. Christians have always been a cantankerous lot,
feuding, fighting, and quarreling over theological questions
that most people do not understand, much less care about.
But the centuries immediately following the peace of the
church in A.D. 313 are among the most tumultuous in the
whole of Christian history. No doubt the passion for controversy during these years is explained in part by the new
status of the church in the empire. No longer did it have to
worry about external enemies; the emperors, who had once
persecuted, had become the protectors, benefactors, and
defenders of the church. Christians could give full attention
to problems within their own ranks. But the controversies of
these centuries also arose because genuine questions had
been raised about cardinal points of Christian faith. Was
Jesus truly God? If he was truly God, how could he also be
truly man? In some cases, these questions were implicit in
earlier Christian thought, but it took several centuries for
their impact to be felt and for them to impress themselves
on the church at large. As men tried to give answers to
these questions, they discovered that the Bible and earlier
tradition did not always give a clear and straightforward
reply. Or, to put it another way, men of equal learning and
reputation learned that on the basis of the same tradition
they came to different conclusions.

## THE PATRISTIC ATTITUDE

The presence of serious differences of opinion on fundamental matters posed something of a dilemma for the church. For centuries, Christians had affirmed that the faith was one, but now at the very time when Christianity was celebrating its newly won status in the empire, Christians discovered that there were many different forms and expressions of this one faith. Differences had existed in earlier times, but now they appeared to assume much greater intensity. It would seem that the need to deal with differences between groups and ideas would have led Christians to recognize the place of diversity within the Christian church but the effect of these controversies was just the reverse. They led to a hardening of attitudes rather than to greater flexibility. If the faith was one, this meant that it had to be the same for everyone at every time and every place.

A relatively unknown bishop Vincent, from Lérins, an island in the Mediterranean off the coast of Cannes, gave classical expression to the patristic attitude in a book called *Commonitorium*. In this work, written in the early part of the fifth century, Vincent set forth the principle that the true and correct faith is "that which has been believed everywhere, always, and by all." By this phrase he meant that, amidst the variety and diversity within the church, there were certain true and authentic teachings that had remained the same from the beginning of Christianity. If one wishes to discover what these teachings are, he has, quite simply, to go out and count Christian heads. For whatever has been believed by *all* Christians, in *every* land, and in *every* age is the true and orthodox faith. Vincent was no fool. He was not saying that all Christians have believed the same things at all times, as though differences did not exist. Vincent realized that many Christians had believed different things. It was because of differing views that he set forth his "canon." The Vincentian canon is a way of dealing with the problem of diversity. Vincent believed that it is on the points where all Christians agree that one will discover the true content of the faith.[4]

When bishops gathered together in council, they believed it was their responsibility to guard and protect this one unchanging faith which they had received through the succession of former bishops. Councils were called to deal with new problems that had arisen and that could not be solved on the basis of existing formulations. The task of the council fathers was to restate the original Christian faith in light of the "heresies which had sprung up." Heresies come and go, but the apostolic faith changes not.

The fathers could not admit changes in the faith, because change implied imperfection. What need is there of alteration if something is perfect to begin with? Differences, then, which might have been viewed as attempts to interpret the Christian faith in light of new conditions, were explained by attributing them to deviation from the one unchanging faith. Since one's own opinions were always thought to have been received through the unbroken apostolic succession and were therefore indubitably orthodox and apostolic, those who differed could only be unorthodox and unapostolic—even if their succession was as certain as anyone else's. No matter how vigorously the bishops disagreed with one another, all assumed that there could be no differences between orthodox Christians. Those who did not agree were by definition heretical. Of course a great part of the difficulty stemmed from the universal belief that the unity of the faith was to be found in dogma. Most Christians would have preferred if all agreed on liturgical matters, church organization, or ecclesiastical practices, but in these areas they could recognize and accept diversity; in the area of dogma, they believed that the oneness of the faith required everyone to confess the same.

If it was not possible to alter the one faith received from the fathers, the most serious charge one could bring against his opponents was the charge of innovation. Obedience to the past and faithfulness to tradition were the most highly praised virtues. The term "innovation," for example, occurs over and over in patristic literature, and it is almost always pejorative. The only time it occurs in a positive context is in connection with the Resurrection of Jesus. Some fathers said that through the Resurrection from the dead, Jesus "innovated a new way for mankind," i.e. he opened up a way that had not been available to men before.[5] But in doctrinal and ecclesiastical controversies the game was to put one's opponents on the defensive by charging them with novelties.

## THE DOCTRINE OF THE TRINITY

The controversies in the fourth century over the doctrine of the Trinity illustrate how the game was played. The issue here was the relation between Jesus Christ and God the Father and, at a later stage in the controversy, the relation between the Holy Spirit and God the Father. In the first stage of the controversy, Athanasius, bishop of Alexandria, and Arius, a priest from the same diocese, were the two chief opponents. Arius took the view that Jesus was to be thought of as divine, but not in the same sense that God the Father was divine. There could be only one God, argued Arius, and if Christ were also God, there would be two gods. Athanasius claimed that Christ, as God's Son, was fully God, of the same substance (*homoousios*) as God the Father. The term *homoousios* could not be found in the Bible and was first used by Christians in the middle of the third century. At the council of Nicaea in A.D. 325, it was given official sanction. "We believe in one God, the Father Almighty, Maker of heaven and earth . . . and in one Lord Jesus Christ, the only Son of God, begotten of his Father, i.e. of the being of the Father, God from God, Light from Light, true God from true God, begotten not made, of one substance (*homoousios*) with the Father by whom all things were made. . . ."[6]

Arius and his supporters branded the council fathers as innovators because they had gone beyond the traditional Christian language to introduce new and unscriptural terms and ideas. Arius considered the conciliar formula *homoousios* an unwarranted departure from apostolic teaching. Athanasius realized the seriousness of the charge and devoted many pages of theological argumentation in defense of the council's action. In a treatise on the Nicene decrees, *De Decretis,* he attempted to justify the new idea by showing that it was a faithful restatement of the apostolic faith handed down in the orthodox churches. At the end of the treatise, Athanasius appends a list of testimonies from earlier teachers to show that what the Fathers proclaimed at Nicaea, ". . . they did not invent themselves, but spoke what they had received from their predecessors. . . ."[7]

Athanasius then returned the compliment by charging Arius with innovation. In a letter written to the bishops in Egypt, Athanasius said, "Therefore, let us, considering that in this struggle everything is at stake, and that the choice is now before us, either to *deny* or to *preserve* the faith, let us make it our earnest care and aim to *guard* what we have received, taking as our instruction the confession drawn up at Nicaea, and let us turn away from *novelties* and teach our people to give heed to 'seducing spirits.' " (emphasis mine)[8] These words, written almost a generation after the council of Nicaea, came from a time in Athanasius' life when he had been exiled from Alexandria and replaced by an Arian bishop. He writes to the bishops of Egypt to defend himself as well as the creed of Nicaea, in the hope of preventing the new bishop from replacing the Nicene Creed with one tailored to Arian doctrine. Athanasius is on the defensive, as he had been for thirty years, for the simple reason that his position represented *one* party in the church and not the universally accepted teaching. On the matter of the Trinity, the church's faith was still in the process of formulation. No one party could make an indisputable claim on Christian truth. Yet neither party could recognize integrity of the other's position. One's opponents were said to be "godless," "impious," "foreign" teachers who shook off the faith of the fathers, and one's own beliefs were thought to be identical with the apostolic faith.[9]

Members of both parties had access to the same apostolic Scriptures. Bishops on opposite sides of issues discovered that their opponents could always find support from the Bible. Since the chief authority in the church was always the Bible, many ecclesiastical controversies frequently became disputes over the correct interpretation of biblical texts. The Bible became the battleground for every important theological controversy in the patristic period. If apostolic origin was the mark of Christian truth, every opinion and every doctrine had to trace its origins to the Bible. Often it took much imagination and ingenuity to discover one's opinions in specific biblical passages, but the fathers were quite up to the task.[10]

The most frequently quoted text in the controversy over the Trinity was a passage from Proverbs 8: "The Lord created me a beginning of his ways for his works" (v. 22). In its original context, the "me" in the passage referred to Wisdom. "My fruit is better than gold, even fine gold, and my yield than choice silver. I walk in the way of righteousness, in the paths of justice, endowing with wealth those who love me, and filling their treasures." To the Christians of the fourth century—Arians and Nicenes—this passage was thought to refer to Christ, who was God's true Wisdom. If Christ is the subject of the passage, thought the Arians, it teaches that Christ was "created." The text says explicitly: "The Lord created me," i.e. Christ. If Christ was created, then he is surely not God, but a creature like other creatures. He was not eternal, for he came into existence at a certain time, i.e. at the time when he was created, and there was a time before he existed, i.e. before he was created. How, then, could he be God?[11]

Athanasius agreed with the Arians that the passage referred to the Son, but he was not at all prepared to accept the view that the passage taught that Christ was a creature. If Proverbs was part of the divinely inspired Scriptures, its teaching had to be in accord with the one unchanging faith. This meant that Proverbs had to agree with the rest of the Scriptures, and they, in Athanasius' view, did not teach that the Son was created. His exegetical assignment was to show how this text could be understood in light of his over-all interpretation of the Scriptures. To do this, Athanasius proposed a number of different ways of understanding Proverbs 8—all designed to avoid the implications drawn by his opponents. We note but one: Athanasius pointed out that, in the Scriptures, the term "create" had many different meanings. For example, in Psalm 51 we read, "Create in me a clean heart, O God, and put a new and right spirit within me." Here, "create" does not mean "come into existence" in the sense that the world came into existence or that man was created; create here refers to the creation of a new heart and spirit in a person who is already living. Athanasius then went on to argue that in Proverbs 8 the term "create" does not refer to the creation of the Son at the beginning of time, i.e. at the creation, but to the new creation of all mankind through the Resurrection of Jesus. The text teaches that, because of Christ's Resurrection, ". . . man no longer walks according to that first creation but there is the beginning of a new creation," and the phrase "beginning of his ways" means that "we follow him who says 'I am the Way.' "[12]

The interpretation of Luke 2:52 posed another exegetical dispute in the fourth century. The text reads: "And Jesus increased in wisdom and in stature, and in favor with God and man." The interpretations of Athanasius and of Arius are contradictory. The Arians took this text to mean that Christ was a man like other men, because he had *advanced* in wisdom in the fashion that all men grow wise and mature. This seemed to be certain proof that Christ was not God. God does not grow or advance in any way, and certainly he does not grow in wisdom. If God is said to advance, this would suggest that he is not perfect and needs to change in order to become perfect. Jesus, however, is not God, said the Arians, and it is proper for the Scriptures to say that he advanced.

Athanasius answers Arius by appealing to an interpretative principle he had worked out earlier in the treatise. According to this hermeneutical key, the Scriptures contain a "double account of the Savior." Some passages refer to Christ in so far as he is God, while others refer to him in so far as he is man. From the former we know "that he was ever God, and is Son, being the Father's Word and Radiance and Wisdom," and from the latter that "afterwards for us he took flesh of a virgin, Mary, bearer of God (*theotokos*), and was made man." If this principle is kept in mind, said Athanasius, the passage from Luke poses no problem. It clearly falls in the latter category. It does not mean that Christ is an ordinary man and therefore that he is not divine; it simply says that when he became man in the womb of the Virgin Mary he took on all the characteristics of a man. Among these characteristics is growth and advancement in wisdom and stature. We say that he advanced, argued Athanasius, in so far as he is man; as God he is always perfect and does not need to grow into maturity or perfection. To say that he advanced means that he imparted his wisdom to men as his life unfolded and he gradually manifested God's grace in ever clearer ways."[13]

The diverse and often contradictory interpretations of the same texts were not due solely to the imagination of theologians and biblical scholars. Neither the Bible, nor tradition for that matter, always spoke with one voice. The very imprecision and ambiguity of the biblical witness on many questions gave room for theological speculation to roam. But it was not only that the Bible itself was not univocal in its message; it was also that the questions men addressed to the Bible were new. The fathers always claimed to be debating the meaning of the original apostolic faith, and their discussions sounded as though they were debates about the past. But the theological controversies of the early church were debates about the *present*. They were an attempt to answer questions and deal with problems raised since apostolic times—problems that were beyond the range of apostolic thinking.

The controversy over the Trinity was not a controversy over the meaning of the Christian faith at the time of the apostles; it was a controversy over issues that had arisen as a result of almost three hundred years of Christian experience. Men began to realize that certain implications of Christian ideas and practices could not be suitably explained on the basis of existing language and conceptions. But the line between a new *expression* or *formulation* and a genuinely new idea or belief was very thin. A new generation of Christians would introduce a new set of terms and expressions to interpret an article of faith, but the new expressions more frequently than not represented new insights which in time *changed* the content of the faith. But the fathers always supported their new, and sometimes revolutionary, ideas by the argument that the new was in fact really the old. Scripture and tradition were the authoritative tests of Christian truth even when they were used to justify "innovations."

### THE HOLY SPIRIT

In a later stage of the Trinitarian controversy, a scenario similar to that at Alexandria and Nicaea was acted out in Cappadocia in Asia Minor. The question now centered about the relation of the Holy Spirit to God the Father. This question had not arisen before the late fourth century, but now that the relation of the Son had been aired so thoroughly in the previous generation, the question of the Holy Spirit's relation to the Father was bound to come up.

The key figures were Basil, bishop of Caesarea; his brother Gregory, bishop of Nyssa; and their close friend Gregory, bishop of Nazianzus. Their chief opponent was Eunomius, bishop of Cyzicus, a town in the province north of Cappadocia. Basil had been born into an aristocratic and wealthy family whose lineage stretched back to the days of persecution under Maximian, Roman emperor at the beginning of the fourth century. Besides Basil, the family of ten included two brothers who became bishops, Peter and Gregory, and a sister, Macrina, who was widely admired for her piety and who exercised a profound spiritual influence on Basil. Basil was fully at home in the orthodox Christian tradition, and never had reason to doubt that what he believed, taught, and practiced was in harmony with the original apostolic faith. "What could be clearer proof of our faith than that we were brought up by our grandmother, a blessed woman . . . by whom we were taught the saying of the most blessed Gregory [bishop of Neocaesarea in the third century] . . . and who moulded and formed us while still young in the doctrines of piety."[14] Anyone with Basil's background would have been horrified to be called an innovator, but this was precisely what happened to him.

Christians had long baptized "in the name of the Father and of the Son and the Holy Spirit," but no one had ever defined precisely whether the Spirit was to be considered fully God. The Bible did not speak of the Holy Spirit as God, Christians seldom addressed prayer to the Spirit, and in popular piety the Spirit was considered third in the hierarchy of being extending from the Father through the

Son to the Spirit. But once the church had taken a definitive stand on the relation of the Son to the Father as it had at Nicaea, some began to ask: what of the Holy Spirit? In an important book on the Holy Spirit and in other writings, Basil took the position that the Holy Spirit is, like the Son, fully God. To the successors of Arius this seemed like the addition of one blasphemy on top of another. Not only is God divided into two by making the Son God, but he is also divided into three by making the Spirit God. What has become of the ancient Christian belief in the unity and oneness of God?

The Arians mounted an attack on Basil because he had introduced a new teaching on the Holy Spirit and destroyed the traditional Christian belief in the oneness of God. "They falsely accuse us," wrote Basil, "of introducing innovations regarding the Holy Spirit. What is our innovation? We confess what indeed we have received. . . ." Basil responds to the charge of innovation by reiterating his conviction that he teaches nothing other than the faith received from the fathers. It is our opponents who are innovators, he writes, for they "have a kind of clever doctrine regarding such changes on their part—that they employ the words of the creed, like physicians, according to occasion, adapting it to their existing conditions now in one way and now in another. . . ." They think we should "compose different creeds at different times and *change* them with the occasion," but if this is so, the words of the Scriptures "One Lord, one faith, one baptism" are false. The business of Christian leaders and theologians is not to invent new beliefs, but to guard the old. We concern ourselves with "no faith except the old. . . . It is sufficient for us to confess what we have received from the Holy Scriptures and to shun innovation to them."[15]

Basil's family may have been orthodox and his ecclesiastical credentials impeccable, but the Arians had a good case against him. They knew that earlier Christian tradition gave him little explicit support for his views, and they also knew the rules of ecclesiastical controversy: antiquity was the sign of truth. They, too, believed that Christians should confess no faith except the old, and they played their trump card against Basil.

Neither Basil nor his opponents was naïve or uninformed about the Christian past. They knew that they lived centuries after the beginning of Christianity; they could see the changes that had taken place over the years. They had also seen the dramatic changes in the relationship between Christianity and the Roman imperium. They could see the differences between Christians in various parts of the Roman world, but in the area of dogma they saw neither diversity nor development. Here they projected a timeless past extending back to the divine revelation given by the Holy Spirit and handed on by later teachers. The apostles handed on one divine truth, and later generations had the responsibility to guard, keep, preserve, and transmit what they have received. The old takes precedence over the new; the past over the present or future.

### THE GROWING IMPORTANCE OF CREEDS

The debates of the fourth and fifth centuries helped to refine the Eusebian construction of the past. As different men faced new situations, they were led inevitably to interpret the faith in new ways. Ever since the beginning of Christianity, Christian teachers, missionaries, bishops, and others had to reinterpret the faith in light of new situations. This can be seen in sermons, catechetical liturgy, biblical exegesis, and in the early creeds. Up to the fourth century, however, most of these efforts were carried on in local areas in light of local conditions, without knowledge of or reference to the larger church. A bishop in Ephesus might have written a simple creed to instruct his catechumens, but he would not have used this creed for any other purpose than to instruct his own converts.

In the fourth and fifth centuries, creeds assumed new importance because they became tests of Christian orthodoxy. The creed issued by the Council of Nicaea was thought to be a standard for the whole church. The older baptismal creeds were, in the words of C. H. Turner, the Anglican church historian, ". . . creeds for catechumens, the new creed [of Nicaea] was a creed for bishops." The older creeds were seldom known outside the locality where they were used, but the new creeds were raised up as universal standards of Christian truth. They became the "touchstone by which the doctrines of Church teachers and leaders might be certified as correct," writes J. N. D. Kelly, one of the authorities on the history of creeds.[16]

This new development led to an extension of apostolic
authority to fixed moments within the Christian past. During the first fifty years after the council of Nicaea, the
decisions of the council were widely contested within
Christendom. By the end of the fourth century and the
beginning of the fifth century, i.e. approximately one hundred years after the council, its decisions were thought to
be identical with the apostolic faith. Anyone who questioned Nicaea was thought to be heretical. In fact, the
fathers went so far as to say that the creed of Nicaea was
given by the Holy Spirit. "We do not allow the faith to be
shaken by anyone," wrote Cyril of Alexandria in the early
fifth century, "for this faith was defined by our holy fathers
who assembled in the time of Nicaea; nor do we permit
either ourselves or others to alter a word or to transgress
a single syllable. . . . For they themselves were not the
speakers, but the Spirit of God."[17] At the council of
Ephesus in 449 the Egyptian bishops expressed the same
conviction: "Let the decisions of the bishops of Nicaea
stand. Let the things of the Holy Spirit stand."

During this same period, Christians also began to ap-
pend long lists of citations from the "holy" fathers to
their theological treatises. Frequently these quotations
were added immediately after lists of biblical texts. The
authority of approved testimonies from the past came to
occupy a place second only to that of the apostles.[18]

Authorities from the past, however, did not always
agree. What had happened with the Bible, now began to
happen with church tradition. The past did not speak
with one voice. Approved voices could be enlisted on

either side of most questions. As different men looked back, they selected those testimonies that supported their views, and overlooked those that did not. Thus began a new game of comparing authorities from the past to answer the problems of the present. If the faith was the same in every generation, there must be witnesses to this unchanging faith in every age.


PETER ABELARD

The Eusebian construction of the past made it difficult for men to see either the diversity of the Christian past or the changes that had taken place over the centuries. By extending the authority of the apostles to later Christian generations, the unity that men had projected onto the first Christian generation, namely that of the apostles, was made to embrace the whole of the Christian past. The irony of the Eusebian view is that in stressing the unity of the tradition—one unchanging faith—it led to a hardening of division and disunity. For if diversity could not be tolerated, the only way of explaining differences was to say that divergent views contradicted or opposed the true faith.

The difficulties of this view were recognized centuries later in the famous book *Sic et Non* (Yes and No), written by Peter Abelard in the twelfth century. In this work he gathered together a list of citations from the fathers on one hundred and fifty questions. He showed that if the teachings of the fathers were placed side by side, they not only diverged sharply; sometimes they actually opposed one another. On many matters of great importance, some fathers gave one answer, i.e. they said "yes"; and others gave quite another answer—they said "no."

Abelard attempted to account for these divergences, but the very solutions he offered showed just how much Christian thinking had been shaped by the Eusebian construction of the past. Abelard suggested that some differences could be explained by false authorship. That is, works that were attributed to an orthodox writer actually were written by a heretic. Others he explained by pointing to retractions later in life, and yet others by the variety of meanings that could be assigned to certain terms. He even suggested that some differences might result from different historical circumstances. What is approved in one generation was sometimes rejected at a later time. But Abelard did not carry through his insight to forge a new interpretation of the Christian past. Instead, he resorted to the notion of authority handed on by the tradition. In the face of genuine contradictions, one should compare authorities, ". . . and the one that is more powerfully attested and has been more fully substantiated is to be preferred." Abelard saw the problem, as Jaroslav Pelikan has observed, not as a question of change and development in the tradition, but as contradiction of an eternal truth. "Abelard's bold recognition of ambiguities in the dogmatic tradition led to an argument in a circle, leaving the relation between theology and change unresolved—or more precisely, resolving it by transposing it into a logical relation. Not change, but contradiction was the key issue."[19]

The inability of the Eusebian construction of the past to recognize change and diversity forced different traditions within Christianity to construct "private" interpretations of the past. If diversity was ruled out, Christians who disagreed with each other on doctrinal matters had no alternative but to separate from their opponents and to exclude them from fellowship. But those whom one excluded were just as capable of justifying their views on the basis of the same Bible and the same tradition. Thus while both claimed to possess the one unchanging truth, they possessed this truth in isolation from one another. The fiction of one truth was kept alive even though the one truth became more splintered with each new crisis in the church's history. To this day, the Coptic church of Egypt, one of the oldest Christian churches in existence, is separated from the rest of Christendom because the Egyptians did not submit to the orthodoxy of the Council of Chalcedon. Nevertheless, both the Copts and the Chalcedonians continue to believe that each possesses the one apostolic faith.

In the course of time, different traditions within Christianity learned to construct their own unique view of the Christian past within the large Eusebian framework. It was possible to provide an interpretation of the Bible that suited one's own views and to single out those segments of the later tradition that appeared to substantiate one's own opinions. Egyptians read the Bible in one way; Romans in another way. Egyptians had their list of approved teachers; the Romans also had theirs. If the apostolic faith was the same in every age, and variation and change were excluded, the only way to deal with differences was to anathematize one's opponents. Inevitably, everyone possessed the true and unchanging faith, but they did not possess it together. It became easy to slay one's opponents by labeling them as innovators and priding oneself on his fidelity to the tradition. There was only one truth, and those who did not embrace this truth were enemies of God. The process by which different traditions within Christianity constructed their own unique form of Christian memory begins in the early church, but its most dramatic expression did not come until the Reformation, in the sixteenth century.

# CHAPTER V

# *The Hateful Charge of Novelty*

WHEN the Reformation burst upon Western Europe, the Eusebian construction of the past still dominated the historical outlook of most Christians. Even though the controversies in antiquity did lead to divisions within the Christian community, and the split between Eastern and Western Christianity in the eleventh century sliced off from the Western church most of the lands where the Christian movement had begun and grown to maturity, it was still possible for Christians in the medieval West to believe that there was one true church, in succession from the apostles, and that this church was the bearer of the true and authentic faith handed down in apostolic times. The Reformation changed all this. Once, differences had existed between individual thinkers, between the tradition of one city or province and another, or between churches in different parts of the world, but now the division was close to home, in the sister church in the next village, in the parish across the river, or in a neighboring duchy. The heretics were neighbors, and they showed no promise of disappearing.

In this situation, the questions arose once again: whose

teaching was apostolic? If the reformers were in control of churches with as much claim to antiquity as the supporters of the pope, how could one tell which was indeed the true church? Not surprisingly, those opposed to reform labeled the reformers "innovators" because they departed from the beliefs and practices men had taken for granted for centuries. But the reformers—no strangers to the gamesmanship of theological controversy—branded the pope and his followers with the same charge. In their view, the church of the sixteenth century had departed from the apostolic faith by introducing many new and unscriptural teachings and practices. If the church was no longer what it had been in apostolic times—and the reformers thought this was apparent—then it must have at one time undergone a change that brought about the perversion and corruption of the present. Therefore, those who are defending the present state of things are innovators, because they accept beliefs and practices that are a deviation from the apostolic model.

### THE HISTORIES OF THE REFORMATION ERA

The Reformation conflict took historical form in two massive historical works conceived and executed during the sixteenth century. The first, a combined effort of a team of Protestant scholars assembled by Matthias Flacius Illyricus, began to appear in 1559; the response, an equally impressive work by the Italian Caesar Cardinal Baronius, began to appear in 1588.

Both books, written in the form of a history of Christianity, reflect to an extraordinary degree the differing attitudes of the two parties in the Reformation. The Protestant view opposed the Roman Catholic by showing that what the Reformers taught was in fact the true and authentic teaching of the true church. To the reformers, this meant that they had to demonstrate where and how their ideas had been expressed in apostolic times, and how they were reaffirmed by approved Christian teachers in the history of the church. The Roman Catholics had to show that the Protestant position had little or no support from the Bible or tradition. What is, however, most striking about the polemics of the Reformation epoch is that underneath the theological differences between Roman Catholics and Protestants, there is a similar historical outlook received from the same tradition. Though their definitions of apostolic orthodoxy diverge sharply, both see the history of Christianity through a similar set of spectacles. Both Protestants and Roman Catholics are in fact Eusebians in a new dress.

Matthias Flacius Illyricus was born in 1520. As a young man, he wished to become a monk, but his uncle, who thought otherwise, sent Matthias to Protestant lands to study. First he went to Basel, then Tuebingen, and eventually Flacius made the pilgrimage to Wittenberg, where he studied with Philip Melanchthon, Luther's colleague and the author of the charter doctrine of the Lutheran Reformation, the Augsburg Confession. Later, he heard Luther himself lecture. For a time, he drifted about from university to university, but eventually he took up residence in Jena and there occupied the chair of New Testament. During these years, he conceived of the idea of a grand history of the church written by a Protestant in defense of the Reformation.


## THE *Centuries*

When the first volume of the *Centuries* appeared in 1559, its scope far transcended any other historical presentation of Christianity up to that time. The centuriators followed an already established pattern of dividing the past into fixed units, but the comprehensiveness of this book had no precedent. Other historians, for example Nauclerus (1430–1510), whose world chronicle, *Memorabilium omnis aetatis et omnium gentium chronici commentarii,* was published posthumously in 1516, divided their histories according to generations; Flacius followed the general pattern, but broke his division down into centuries. What singled out the *Centuries,* however, was the subdivisions in each century. To avoid reducing ecclesiastical history either to doctrine, history of institutions, history of heresy, of persecution or of mission, the authors of the *Centuries* tried, by their divisions, to comprehend the whole range of experience within the Christian tradition. Each century was divided into sixteen sections: general characteristics of the age, the expansion of the church, persecution and peace, i.e. the eternal situation of the church, doctrines, heresies, ceremonies and rites, polity and government of the church, schisms, councils, notable persons, heretics, martyrs, miraculous events, Judaism, other religions, and political history.

No history of Christianity before the *Centuries* was as broad in its conception of the task, and few since have been equal to the ideal projected by Flacius and his colleagues. The division of history into centuries and the subdivision of each century into sixteen divisions obviously had some drawbacks, chiefly because it tended to draw arbitrary lines in interpreting the material. Not everything in every century was of equal importance: at times, doctrinal questions may dominate the stage; at a later date, the relation of the church to the state; and at another time, persecution. Not every century lent itself to a division into sixteen parts. The basic intention, however, is sound, as an incentive for the historian to search out significant as well as insignificant material in each period, and to encourage him to keep before himself a large vision of the total Christian experience.[1]

The somewhat wooden outline of the *Centuries* into divisions of one hundred years, and the fixed set of topics, do not mean that the work is simply a detached presentation of the story of the Christian past. The centuriators of Magdeburg are clearly interpreting the past for the uses of the present. Flacius had set forth his historical program in an earlier work, the *Catalogus testium veritatis,* in which he argued that there had always been men in the history of Christianity who "cried out against the Roman pontiff and his errors." In this book, Flacius wished by his choice of testimonies to point to those who have stood fast against error and defended the truth. In the course of centuries, as the popes assumed greater powers, the witness of these men had been forgotten. We wish, then, wrote Flacius, to show that the "sophistry of the papists is false," for it tries to "attribute to us and to our religion the *hateful charge of novelty* [emphasis mine] and to attribute to themselves the dignity of great age." The Protestants, good Eusebians, wished, like their opponents, to envelop their teachings in the cloak of antiquity.[2]

The preface to the *Centuries* enumerates three uses (*utilitatae*) that prompt the writing of ecclesiastical history.

1. It is an article of faith that the catholic church is preserved in every age and that the church will continue by God's grace through the ministry of the Word of God. The historian has the responsibility of showing God's presence in the actual course of events.

2. Apostolic doctrine remains the same in every age, for there is only one faith. "The article of the heavenly teaching never changes but always remains the same," wrote the centuriators.

3. The earliest teaching is truest, and the teachings of the reformers are "not new, but old [*illa ipsa vetus, non nova*]."[3]

From the viewpoint of the reformers, the church of the sixteenth century was, by the very abuses it condoned, a living testimony that the papal church had made additions to the faith and departed from the apostolic testimony. If the church as it appeared in the sixteenth century was not faithful to the apostles, somewhere in the course of sixteen centuries there had been a falling away from apostolic Christianity. The logic of the Protestant position demanded some sort of "fall of the church" theory. Eusebius had not spoken of a fall of the church, but the metaphor of virginity lent itself readily to the Protestant view. In the Reformation historiography, the idea of a fall of the church provided a historical conception to account for the discrepancy Protestants saw between late medieval Christendom and the apostolic church they read of in the New Testament. To justify their teaching, they had to explain how it could be that an apparently new teaching, justification through faith by grace, was in fact the original and true apostolic doctrine. They argued that justification had been taught by the apostles, it had been lost in later generations, and now it had been discovered again.

The reformers knew that their case was fragile if they could only show that justification by grace was taught in apostolic times, for, if there were no witnesses between the apostles and the reformers to this teaching, their opponents could claim that they had misunderstood the apostolic writing. It was, in short, not sufficient to demonstrate the apostolicity of justification by faith, if there were no reliable witnesses in the intervening years.

Melanchthon, from whom Flacius got many of his ideas, preached a sermon at Luther's death. In this sermon, he addressed this question directly and unrolled a list of witnesses to the true faith: Adam, Seth, Enoch, Methusaleh, Noah, Sem, Moses, Joshua, Samuel, David, Elias, Elijah, Isaiah, Jeremiah, Daniel, Zachariah, Esdras, Onias, Simeon, John the Baptist, Christ, apostles, Polycarp, Irenaeus, Gregory of Neocaesarea, Basil, Augustine,

Prosper, Maximus, Hugo, Bernard, Tauler, and finally
Luther. The historical construction of the *Magdeburg
Centuries* takes its cue from this list of faithful witnesses.
The church was founded by the apostles, and their teaching was deposited in the New Testament writings. New
and strange teachings lead men away from the apostolic
doctrine of justification, but God, through faithful witnesses, keeps alive the memory of this teaching even
though errors continue to spread. The remnant perseveres
amidst error and apostasy until the day that the true light
of the gospel is again allowed to shine forth.[4]

Eusebius lived before the papacy had become the chief
ruling power in the church of the West. He recognized
the importance of the bishop of Rome, but, in the history,
the bishop of Rome plays no singular role. By the sixteenth century, however, the bishop of Rome had become, for the Western church, the chief guarantor of the
apostolic tradition. The centuriators reserve their biggest
guns for the papacy. To answer the question "Why did the
apostolic faith almost disappear?" the centuriators single
out the papacy as the primary cause. In their reading of
the Christian past, the papacy becomes not the guarantor
of the tradition, but the innovator par excellence. For
the first two centuries, the pope lay in hiding, according
to the centuriators, but by the third century the "mystery
of iniquity" began to rear its head, and with each passing
century he became more bold, more dangerous, and more
open in his attacks on the gospel and additions to the
apostolic faith. Gleefully the centuriators parade forth the
sins of the papacy. Unfortunately the bias of the authors

is so pronounced that they abandon their own critical principles to accept legend and fabricated documents without careful examination. They accept, for example, the legend of the female pope Joan, supposedly elected in 855, and make of her a symbol of the degeneracy of the papacy. "In this century [ninth] God had revealed by a marvelous and conspirous deed the baseness of the pontifical see and has exposed the Babylonian harlot to the eyes and gaze of all, so that the pious might recognize that holy pontifical dignity which was held in reverence by the whole world, to be the mother of all fornication, spiritual and corporeal, and learn to curse and detest her."[5]

Attacks on the papacy serve the larger purpose of placing the light of Luther's teaching against the dark background of papal escapades. As the reader gradually senses the darkness that shrouded the church, he is supposed to see more clearly the brilliance of the light of the Reformation gospel. To this end, the *Centuries* dwells at length on the changes and alterations in apostolic teaching from the time of the apostles to Luther. Change in the *Magdeburg Centuries,* as it was in the history of Eusebius, can only be change for the worse. At no other time in the history of Christianity was the divine truth so clearly revealed as in the apostolic age and again in the sixteenth century. Church history has the task of presenting before the reader the career of this faith as it has lived on till the present day. In the historiography of the reformers, wrote Ferdinand Christian Baur, the old Eusebian notion remains intact, for "in the entire historical sequence of the church everything remains as it was from the beginning, and no change can take place by which the substantial forms of the church might be substantially altered."[6]

In the *Magdeburg Centuries* the chief part of ecclesiastical history was doctrine, though the chief doctrine was no longer the divinity of Christ, as in Eusebius, since this is assumed by both the reformers and their opponents. The chief doctrine was justification by grace through faith. In Reformation theology, the chief article of justification extended into every phase of Christian thought and piety, and the centuriators were able to use this central idea as a critical principle to interpret the whole of church history. The centuriators had no qualms about placing the precise language and terminology of the reformers into the mouths of the apostles. Even Christ himself spoke Luther's language. We often hear from Christ, they wrote, of the "gracious goodness and the beneficent release from the evil of the law for the sake of Christ" and of the "gracious imputation of righteousness through the blood of Christ." The benefits of God's grace are "imputed because of the merit of Christ," and Christ assures believers of "remission of sins or imputation of justice and salvation, not by human works either in part or wholly . . . but only by his own beneficence and merit and grace." Most of these terms and phrases occur in a technical sense in the writings of the reformers. The whole of Christian experience was seen through the spectacles of justification by grace through faith. The result is highly effective polemics, but somewhat dubious history.[7]

THE *Annales Ecclesiastici*

The *Magdeburg Centuries* was, however, a historical
work, and it called for a historical reply. Rome saw immediately that another history of Christianity was the only
adequate response. The mantle fell on a very young man,
Caesar Baronius, born in Naples in 1538, some twenty
years after the posting of the 95 Theses. When selected
to take over the task of answering the *Centuries,* Baronius
was only twenty-one years old, but he saw immediately
that the Roman response would have to be as monumental
in conception and as thorough in execution as the *Centuries*. Baronius was too intelligent to believe that he could
simply dash off a polemical tract exposing the errors of
the centuriators. Like Flacius, he set his mind and energies
to the study of the past. His *magnum opus* would be a
history, not a polemical or dogmatic essay. For thirty
years, he worked amidst the rich resources of the Vatican
archives before he began to publish the *Annales Ecclesiastici*. Patiently he did the work of a historian—gathering
and editing manuscripts, collecting materials, sifting the
remains of antiquity, critically analyzing suspicious texts,
weeding out the myths and legends accumulated over centuries. His first volume did not appear until thirty years
after the publication of the first volume of the *Centuries* and fifteen years after the last volume of the *Centuries* was published.

Baronius, like present-day politicians in a campaign,
did not give his opponents the pleasure of calling them

by name, but his target is clear enough. The use of history, he wrote, was to promote "piety and virtue" by the inspiration of the fathers and saints, but the history presented here also has a further purpose. We intend here to direct our attention "especially against the innovators of our time" and to defend the "antiquity of the sacred tradition and the power of the holy Roman Catholic Church."[8] Baronius, too, believed that antiquity was a mark of truth. In place of the florid prose and great artistry of many histories, especially ancient histories, whose style was as important as content, Baronius proposed to write a history devoted to historical truth and accuracy, a non-partisan account of the Christian past. Even the title, *Annales,* Baronius thought, showed the objectivity of the work; for in contrast to a story told by centuries, Baronius wished to present his history year by year. Only then can one hope to record faithfully what took place.

Baronius is no less partisan than Matthias Flacius Illyricus, but his construction of the past breathes a different spirit. Whereas the tone of the *Centuries* is frequently gloomy and pessimistic as the decline of the church unfolds before the reader, Baronius creates an impression of steadfastness, constancy, and perseverance as the church weathers each new storm. Both the *Centuries* and the *Annales,* however, agree that there is no place for legitimate change within the Christian faith. The *Centuries* ruled out change because approval of change would legitimate the alterations brought by the papacy; Baronius allows no room for change for he wishes to show that the institutions present in the church at the time of the Reformation

were established by Christ and have been faithfully per-
petuated by the successors of the apostles up to the present. Whereas Flacius tends to play up discontinuity,
Baronius accents continuity. The original foundation has
endured. Our task, wrote Baronius, is "to demonstrate
through successive periods that the visible monarchy of
the Catholic Church was established by Christ the Lord,
was founded upon Peter, and through his legitimate and
true successors, the Roman pontiffs, was preserved invio-
late, was guarded scrupulously, and was never broken or
interrupted but perpetually maintained; and that there has
always been recognized one visible head of this mystical
body of Christ, the church, whom all members obey."[9]

The *Annales* comes off better as a historical work than
the *Centuries,* partly because Baronius had the advantage
of studying the *Centuries* before he wrote his book, but
also because Baronius is not so preoccupied with one
theological idea. An institution, e.g. the papacy, gives the
historian a lot more room to breathe than an idea. The
story of the fortunes of the bishop of Rome is a grand
theme for any historian. What more could one ask than
fifteen centuries of one institution whose power and influence extended around the Western world, popes who
toppled mighty kings and proud emperors, who contended
with pernicious error, who lived in poverty and squalor in
the sixth century, who crowned Charlemagne in the ninth,
who sat with princes in elegant palaces in Renaissance
splendor, and who shared the glory of the eternal city?
Baronius' history is more interesting for the simple reason

that Baronius' subject is vulnerable to history in a way that Flacius' was not. No matter what happened or what might happen, the centuriators could retreat into the security of the idea of justification, claiming that the visible church had gone underground, leaving only a remnant, but one day it would surface again. The papacy, seemingly more secure, lived a much more precarious existence, for it could be destroyed.

### ONE CERTAIN TRUMPET

Both Flacius and Baronius sought and found one certain trumpet in the whole history of Christianity. The Protestants preferred the theological idea of justification by grace through faith, and the Roman Catholics preferred an institution—the papacy. As heirs to the Eusebian model of history, the authors of both the *Centuries* and the *Annales* present the Christian past as a conflict between apostolic Christianity, i.e. the true and unchanging faith as each conceived it, and its foes. The Eusebian model remained intact. However, the Reformation prompted the Roman Catholics to reconsider the claims they had made about the past, and Baronius, in turn, forced the Protestants to do the same. It was becoming apparent now not only that some of the supports for either position were not bolstered by sound historical evidence, but that there was at least one other way of interpreting the Christian past. In the polemics that followed the Reformation in the late sixteenth and seventeenth centuries, partisans of both sides had to return again and again to historical questions because their adversaries used historical arguments to support their claims.

Neither the *Centuries* nor the *Annales* was ready to grant the legitimacy of another interpretation of the past. Each thought there was only one way of looking at things, and each, in turn, thought that those who disagreed were dangerous innovators. But the very fact that there were now *two* histories made a difference. The heretics and innovators, with equally impressive historical erudition and theological credentials, were now in the bosom of the church, and they wielded as clever a pen as their opponents. Heretics were no longer a memory from the past or tiny sects set off from the rest of the church. They were very much present, and their ideas had taken institutional form in other Christian communions making similar claims about faithfulness to the apostolic traditions and the fathers. This was to make a difference.

## CHAPTER VI

# *Apostles at Your Service*

IF the apostles could speak Luther's German and the Pope's Latin at the same time, it was a sure bet they would soon learn a few other languages. Luke's account of the gift of tongues to the apostles at Pentecost was coming true in a new and unexpected way. For centuries, men thought the apostles knew only one language, the language of Roman orthodoxy, but the reformers showed that, with imagination and a fresh look at the biblical writings, the apostles could be made to speak not of popes, indulgences, and works, but of grace, faith, and the priesthood of believers. At first the new language sounded barbaric to the defenders of the tradition, but the reformers replied that the reason it sounded so foreign was that the pope and bishops had forgotten the language of the church's infancy. Both—reformers and their opponents—claimed to speak the purer tongue; both thought they knew what the true and original Christian speech sounded like. Nevertheless, something new had happened. The Christian nation had become bilingual. Each party may not have liked what he heard spoken by his neighbors, but no one could overlook any longer the others' presence.

If the apostles could speak the language of Roman and
Protestant orthodoxy with equal facility, why could they
not learn other languages? Placed at the service of
theological controversy and apologetics, the study of the
Christian past became a standard part of the repertoire of
dogmatic and polemical writings in the period following
the Reformation. As the fathers of the fourth and fifth centuries had once combed the Scriptures and the tradition
for just the right quotations and choice illustrations to buttress their arguments, Protestants and Roman Catholics
now went back to the same sources to illustrate, bolster,
and defend their competing claims about Christian truth.
Many polemical works read like treatises in the history
of dogma. One by-product of the controversies of this age
was a deeper historical consciousness, engendered by the
extensive examination of the past. Inevitably some men
—the more reflective and curious—went on to more wide-
ranging historical study. The search for manuscripts, the
editing and publishing of texts, and the development of
critical tools for understanding and interpreting these
texts were not lost simply on the polemics of the moment. These labors bore fruit in fine critical editions of
the early Christian writers, perceptive historical studies,
and a greater awareness of the variety, diversity, and
richness of the Christian past.

### THE LEFT-WING REFORMERS

Protestants and Roman Catholics viewed the Christian
past in language both could understand. They may not

have agreed on the definition of orthodox Christianity, but they prized the apostolic age and the later tradition for similar reasons. The Reformation did not lead to a fundamental re-evaluation of the traditional Christian view of the past. But Luther, Calvin, and other "churchly" reformers were not the only reformers in the sixteenth century. The so-called "left-wing" reformers went much further in their criticism of the tradition and in their interpretation of the Christian past. The Anabaptists (literally, "baptized over again"), for example, rejected the established Christian practice of baptizing children as infants. They urged a second baptism, i.e. a rebaptism when the child reached maturity. They not only questioned the claims of the Roman papacy, as had the other reformers, but they also questioned accepted beliefs and practices untouched by the other reformers, as for example, traditional attitudes about an ordered ministry, the Eucharist, and in some cases even the Christian doctrine of the Trinity.

It is difficult to generalize about the Anabaptists, or the "radical reformers" as George Huntston Williams has called them, but there are certain characteristic marks that set them off from Luther, Calvin, Zwingli, and others. The radical reformers believed in the separation of their churches from the national or territorial state; they denounced war and the use of force; they insisted on believers' baptism; they believed in the possession of the gifts of the Spirit in all Christians, not primarily or solely in an office such as the priesthood; and they gave a

prominent place to the experience of personal regenera-
tion. In the radical reformers, the inner illumination by
the Holy Spirit was always thought to be more significant than an appeal to an authoritative past tradition.[1]

What we know from the writings of these reformers on
church history—largely through statements in polemical,
devotional, and exegetical works—indicates that in most
respects they did not construct a new view of the Christian past in light of their new understanding of the Christian faith. They rather adopted the Eusebian model, but
in a more radical dress. They pushed the time of the "fall
of the church" back almost into the apostolic era, for example, and branded even the traditional creeds and dogmas
as a sign of the church's corruption. They saw the institu-
tionalization of the church during the first few centuries
as another sign that the freedom and enthusiasm of the
apostolic age had been replaced by the tyranny of popes
and bishops. They saw no evidence for infant baptism in
the New Testament, and used this datum as proof that
their practice of baptizing adults conformed to the apostolic model. In some respects, however, they departed from
the traditional pattern by giving an impressive place in
their thinking to the role of the present age in the church's
history. This age, for them of course the sixteenth century, was thought to be the beginning of a new era when
the trappings of authoritative, hierarchial, dogmatic religion would give way to the age of the Spirit, when all
believers would be enlightened by the brightness of the
Spirit.

PIETISM

These ideas, however, did not issue in a major historical work such as the *Magdeburg Centuries*. The right-wing reformers and the papal historians dominate the historiography of the Reformation. In the seventeenth and eighteenth centuries, within Protestantism, we see the first attempts at a more fundamental re-evaluation of the writing of the Christian past. The doctrinal controversies of the Reformation era led, after a time, to a gradual stultification and hardening of the insights of the Reformation. The seventeenth century, the age of Protestant scholasticism, was a time when clergy and theological professors devoted their theological efforts to a codification of the inheritance from the Reformation and to seemingly endless controversies with Roman Catholic polemicists. Not unexpectedly, many Protestant churches began to realize that the churches that had inherited the Reformation were themselves in need of reform. The reform movement was called Pietism.

Originally, Pietism began as an attempt to revive the churches by devotional meetings in homes, Bible study, and prayer, but in a very short time its leaders were able to mount a vigorous offensive against the established clergy, the administrators of the churches, and the theological professors who had inundated the churches with their enormous theological tomes. The founder of the Pietist movement, Philipp Jacob Spener (1635–1705), was a German pastor who believed that the churches in

Germany had forsaken the true spirit of the Reformation. In a little book published in 1675, *Pia Desideria,* he set forth a series of proposals for breathing new life into the churches, as well as a spirited criticism of the widespread corruption of the churches. Spener laid blame on the clergy, civil authorities, church officials, and what he called the "common people." If one looks at the lives of Christians, said Spener, he will discover that while most live an outward life of morality that appears blameless, inwardly most of these people are driven by a "wordly spirit." The churches claim to profess the true faith and to proclaim God's word in their pulpits, but if one observes how supposedly "true" Christians live, he will see at once that many are "unacquainted with the true, heavenly light and the life of faith."[2]

Spener blamed the decline of the life of faith in part on the inordinate preoccupation of the clergy with theological disputation and controversy. Though it is not correct to say, thought Spener, that doctrinal questions are unimportant, it is just as incorrect to think that the possession of the proper opinions is the chief part of Christian faith. "Doctrinal orthodoxy" is not the only mark of true Christianity. "Controversies are not the only or the most important thing, although knowledge of them properly belongs to the study of theology. Not only should we know what is true in order to follow it, but we should also know what is false in order to oppose it. However, not a few stake almost everything on polemics. They think that everything has turned out very well if only they know how to give answer to the errors of the papists, the Reformed, the

Anabaptists, etc. They pay no attention to the fruits of those articles of faith which we presumably still hold in common with them or of those rules of morality which are acknowledged by us all."[3] The proper aim of the study of Christian doctrine, then, is not to refute one's opponents or to show the truth of one's own point of view; theology's aim is the practice of piety.

Gottfried Arnold (1666–1714), a church historian and follower of Spener, saw the possibilities of a history of Christianity written from this new perspective. Arnold, like most Pietists, was as impatient with the orthodoxy of his own Lutheran churches as he was with the orthodoxy of Roman Catholicism. What was the value of having the true Christian doctrine if it did not issue in a life of genuine piety? Whether one revered the orthodoxy of the Augsburg Confession or that of the Council of Trent made little difference to Arnold. What mattered was how men lived. He had seen the fruits of both Lutheran and Roman doctrinal purity in his day, and he did not like what he saw. While men quarreled over minute points of doctrine, wrote learned tomes on the chief articles of faith, and worshiped before the altar of the apostolic faith, the churches were in disarray, men had gone in search of gods of the mind, of ambition, of power. The churches had abandoned the life of faith and devotion. Why not support the reform of the church by writing a history of Christianity whose theme was Christian piety?

His book, *Non-Partisan Church History and History of Heretics from the Beginning of the New Testament to the Year of Christ 1688,* rejected out of hand the traditional identification between orthodoxy and piety.[4] Arnold showed that some of the revered fathers of the church who were doctrinally pure in their theological works were scoundrels as persons and as churchmen, and that some of the most pious, devout, and faithful Christians were not doctrinally sound. Even heretics often lived more God-pleasing lives than the church fathers. Arnold took the daring step of making heretics the heroes of his history. Judged by the standard of piety, many orthodox bishops had no genuine spirituality, and many of the heretics who were condemned by these same bishops showed greater love for their fellows and more fervent devotion to God than the proud judges who sat in councils or issued decrees from Rome. Because Arnold was a Lutheran, he tended to agree with the *Centuries* on more historical points than he agreed with the *Annales,* but the uniqueness of his work was that he based his judgments on a completely different set of principles.

His treatment of Athanasius and the controversies of the ancient church illustrate his approach. Both the *Centuries* and the *Annales* had praised Athanasius as an unambiguous symbol of orthodoxy and a defender of the true faith. But Athanasius was also a ruthless and vindictive church politician. Why should one approve Athanasius and condemn his opponents if Athanasius has nothing more to his credit than his doctrinal orthodoxy? What Athanasius thought about the *homoousios* of Nicaea was to Arnold less important than the effect this doctrine had on his life. By Arnold's standards, many of the churchmen of the fourth century lacked the essentials of true

Christian piety. Orthodox Christian doctrine may have been victorious, but the age of Constantine was a time when Christian leaders lusted for power, and instead of thanking God for their new freedom, they spent their time fighting over points of dogma, and themselves became the persecutors of heretics. "True and active faith no longer had a place, and religion consisted of certain concepts and terms invented by reason, as well as of outward oral confessions and other works performed without faith. Whoever could adapt himself properly to the accepted way, and not doubt the already firmly established authority and power of the bishops, was called orthodox; he might or might not have been an upright Christian. But whoever could not find all their sentences, opinions, and artificial words in the Bible, or otherwise could not regard them as acceptable with conviction of conscience, must be called a heretic. Thus the majority of the people fell into wickedness and dependence on the most external crutches, such that there was often little to distinguish them from pagans."[5]

A NEW CRITICAL PRINCIPLE

Arnold introduced a new critical principle for viewing the Christian past. Piety, not doctrine, was the mark of true Christianity. But he still retained something of the older model. Neither the papacy nor justification by faith served as his standard, but, like his immediate predecessors, Arnold still believed that there was *one* ideal, one standard, that can serve to interpret the whole of Christian history. Christianity itself always remains the same, and in every period we can judge the particular form of Christianity at that time in the light of what, ideally, the Christian church ought always to be. "There are new actors, but still a single pageant,"[6] wrote Arnold. Arnold also derived his standard from what he considered to be the form of Christianity in apostolic times. Though he prized the apostles for different reasons from those of the centuriators or Baronius, it was still the apostles who defined the true marks of the church. He criticized church fathers, bishops, and popes, but he did not criticize the apostles. The apostolic age was still the golden age, and the true expression of the faith was to be sought there. The corruptions of the church did not come until later. Just as the apostles had learned to speak the language of the sixteenth-century reformers over a century earlier, now they learned to speak the language of Spener's *Pia Desideria,* the language of seventeenth-century Pietism. But though the vocabulary changed, the logic of the older view persisted.

Arnold's work is nevertheless epoch-making. Even though he clung to the traditional scheme and made the apostolic age normative for every later age, his unusual and eccentric interpretation of the Christian past helped to shatter the unity men had projected onto the past. Even the orthodox Christian tradition was beginning to appear less monolithic than men had once thought. Protestants and Roman Catholics frequently appealed to the same authors to support their conflicting points of view, but now Arnold had demonstrated that yet another reading of the same history was possible. The Christian faith had not only taken many different forms in the course of its history, but now rival interpretations of this past were becoming available in historical studies.

The eighteenth century and early nineteenth century was one of the most creative periods in the history of the writing of church history.[7] Traditional dogmatic patterns of thought were giving way to historical ideas, and men began to realize that beliefs handed on in the churches as eternal truth may, on examination, turn out to be little more than several centuries old. Some began to see that it was possible to view Christian doctrines in the light of their historical development and not simply in light of their divine origin. The study of the Christian past impressed Christian thinkers with the variety and diversity of Christianity, just as it had once impressed men with its unity. The principle of Vincent of Lérins, "what has been believed everywhere, at all times, and by everyone," as a test of Christian teaching became less and less credible. Where earlier historians saw one unchanging faith handed down from generation to generation, a new generation saw every age as unique, with its own contributions to make to the growth of Christian beliefs and institutions. Church historians of the eighteenth century celebrated the heterogeneity of the Christian past.

## THE "FATHER OF *Dogmengeschichte*"

Johann Salomo Semler (1725–91) was the most brilliant representative of this new historical consciousness.

Sometimes called the "father of *Dogmengeschichte*" (historical theology), Semler, in numerous studies of the Bible and the history of Christianity, waged a vigorous polemic against the authoritarian use of the Christian past characteristic of most theological—and historical—literature of his day. He had been influenced by Siegmund Jacob Baumgarten (1706-57), a systematic theologian, and shortly after Baumgarten's death, Semler edited Baumgarten's *Evangelical Dogmatics* with a preface entitled "Some Comments and a Historical Introduction by Johann Salomo Semler." The "some comments" by Semler actually comprise several hundred pages. In this introduction, he argues that if we look carefully at the records from the Christian past we discover that there were different ideas from the very beginning of Christianity. As the Christian community grew and reflected on the traditions received from the previous generations, and later as these traditions became codified in the New Testament, different men came to the Scriptures with differing experiences and differing temperaments, sensitivities, and intellectual outlooks. These varying experiences shaped the way different men interpreted the Scriptures. Because men came to the Scriptures with different outlooks and experiences—what Semler called different types of "natural revelation"—they developed differing conceptions about God and the chief articles of Christian faith.[8]

Semler saw that if no man stands in precisely the same relation to the Scriptures as another, none will believe precisely the same thing, and more importantly, none can claim to have grasped an eternal truth that was supposed to be imbedded in the Scriptures.

"I in fact begin by holding it to be untrue that such a firm determinate description of Christian truths or concepts is contained in the Bible that only a single conception must and ought to be the true conception forever, as has been taught so long. I must regard it as a theological theory that was authoritative for a certain period of time, and that is also valid for the purpose of an outwardly united religious society, and for the sake of common outward aims; at any one time there can be only one dominant public language in a society. But for the authentic inner religion it is not valid, it is not possible."[9]

Each age has its own responsibility to forge its own distinctive meaning of the Christian faith. The work of one generation or epoch cannot claim to embody an unchanging conception of the true meaning of Christian faith. From his investigations, Semler drew the conclusion that we cannot uncritically accept the opinions of former teachers, no matter how venerable, for they are witnesses not to an eternal truth but to the form Christian thought and practice assumed in response to the demands of different ages. Each age has its own strengths and weaknesses, its own accomplishments and failures. How can the work of one generation become the standard to judge another?

The developments in historical thinking during the late eighteenth and nineteenth centuries, symbolized here by the work of Semler, gave to Christian thinking ever since that time a new series of theological questions. Eusebius had been aware of the variety within the Christian tradition, but his theological perspective provided no way for him to interpret this variety except as a deviation from the accepted norms. Eusebius wrote his history on the assumption of the unity of the Christian tradition. Because he began with the conception of uniformity and the conviction that all things authentically Christian remained the same (*semper eadem*), and because he had no competition from fellow historians in different Christian communions, he did not have to come to terms with the problem of diversity and change. Modern historians, however, begin at just the other end of the spectrum. With every new advance in historical science, they have to give greater place to the dissimilarities they discover in the Christian past, to the contrasts and contradictions, to heterogeneity, originality, and novelty. For the modern historian, the problem presented by the study of church history is not, How do I account for the changes? but, How, in light of the change, do I account for the continuity? Put in other terms: How does one explain that the movement that began in Palestine in the first century, and now found in China, Poland, Egypt, Italy, and the United States, is the *same?*

### THE INFALLIBLE BIBLE

When the impact of historical thinking was greatest and the problem of historical relativity most acute, many Christians took refuge in some form of absolutism. Protestants, more thoroughgoing Eusebians than Roman

Catholics, made of the Bible the only sure bulwark against the shifting sands of historical development. The Reformation had prepared the way for Protestant biblicism by pitting the Bible against tradition, but in the nineteenth century the authority of the Bible assumed a greater role in the Protestant consciousness. Historical study had shown just how unreliable tradition could be as a guide—tradition kept changing, but the Bible was unchanging. To be sure, the way people understood the Scriptures changed with the passage of time, but the Bible enshrined the original faith, and with careful scholarship one can get back to the original meaning of the Scriptures. Indeed, the same historical methods used to demolish the argument from tradition were now enlisted in support of the authority of the Bible. When all else passes away, the Bible stands as a firm foundation for Christianity.

With the rise of Darwinism, Christians saw the Bible threatened from yet another quarter. Not only did historical scholarship dispute the accuracy of the biblical record; now scientific discoveries had undercut the Bible's account of the origin of the world. If Darwin's hypothesis is true, wrote the *American Quarterly Church Review* in 1865, "then is the Bible 'an unbearable fiction,' fabricated during successive ages," and Christians have been "duped by a monstrous lie" for almost two thousand years. Many Christians responded by simply reasserting the infallibility of the Bible. "The Bible is the word of God," said Charles Hodge, the distinguished Presbyterian theologian at Princeton Theological Seminary in 1872. "If granted, then it follows that what the Bible says, God says. That ends the matter."[10] Even today, one can find tiny tracts in the narthexes of some churches with a picture of a pretty, white, colonial-style church building perched on a large, solid, blackbound King James Bible.

## THE INFALLIBLE POPE

Roman Catholics, on the other hand, opted for an institution. The polemics of several centuries taught the Roman Catholics that the only real defense against Protestant criticism, especially as it became sophisticated about historical questions, was not an appeal to an infallible Bible, but to an infallible pope. The Protestants had enough historical evidence on their side to make the Roman claims difficult to defend, just as the Roman Catholics had enough evidence to expose the Protestant claims. It does not take a great deal of historical knowledge to realize that the papacy did not exist in apostolic times, nor to realize that justification by grace through faith is not the leitmotiv that holds together the whole of Christian doctrine from apostolic times to the present. Neither Protestant nor Catholic could rely on tradition alone. In the papacy, Roman Catholics had an institution that could improve on the tradition, alter the tradition, and even introduce novelties, while claiming that the innovations were faithful to the apostolic deposit. No matter what the Bible or tradition seemed to say, the present pope was the authentic interpreter of the tradition. "I am tradition," Pio Nono (Pius IX) was reported to have said. The papacy alone had access to the true meaning of the apostolic faith.

In theological circles, the growing awareness of historical change gave rise to the search for an essence of Christianity. If Christianity was constantly changing, there must be one idea, one principle or essence, which expressed the true character of Christianity. For if there is no such essence, how does one know whether any given form of Christianity is true to the original Christian faith? How can one know whether he truly speaks the word of God? The Eusebian view lived on in modern times under a new guise. Its new expression stated that one could discover an idea or principle to express the true meaning of Christianity "everywhere, always, and by everyone," that this idea was latent in the apostolic writings, and that it was authoritative for later Christian generations. Various forms of the "essence" theory also found historical expression.

### JOHN HENRY NEWMAN

John Henry Newman's theory of doctrinal development is the most widely known solution to the problem of historical change. Newman began where the historians of his day had left him. There was no need to argue that the Christianity of the nineteenth century, whether Protestantism, Anglicanism, or Roman Catholicism, is not identical with the Christianity of the apostolic age. There is discrepancy between ancient Christianity and every variety of modern Christianity. "The Vincentian Canon (Vincent of Lérins), wrote Newman, "true as it must be considered in the abstract, is hardly available now or effective of any satisfactory result. The solution it offers is as difficult as the original problem."[11] Newman could not overlook the changes he saw in the history of Christianity. In doctrine, in polity, in liturgy and sacraments, and in customs, the Christian past is an exuberant garden whose colors and textures are as manifold as those of the rainbow. He was not particularly troubled by changes in organization or liturgy, since he recognized that any human community experiences development in these areas. What concerned him was doctrine, however, a sign that the Eusebian viewpoint is still very much alive in his thinking.

I am willing to admit, writes Newman, "that there are in fact certain apparent variations in its [the church's] teaching which have to be explained." My argument is that the "increase and expansion of the Christian creed and ritual, and the variations which have attended the process in the case of individual writers and church are the necessary attendants on any philosophy or polity which takes possession of the intellect and heart, and has had any wide or extended dominion; that from the nature of the human mind, time is necessary for the full comprehension and perfection of great ideas; and that the highest and most wonderful truths, though communicated to the world once for all by inspired teachers, could not be comprehended all at once by the recipients, but as being received and transmitted by minds not inspired and through media which were human, have required only the longer time and deeper thought for their full elucidation. This may be called the Theory of Development of Doctrine."[12]

Newman's theory is an attempt to account for the continuity of an original "idea" from apostolic times through the manifold changes occurring within Christian experience. Is it possible to show how this idea assumed different forms in the course of time without losing its original and authentic Christian character? His purpose is to justify on historical grounds, in response to the attacks on Catholicism, the mid-nineteenth-century Roman Catholic church as the rightful inheritor of the apostolic faith.

Viewed in light of our discussion of the Eusebian construction of the past, the following points are worth observing.

1. Newman distinguishes the "idea" of Christianity from its development. The chief idea of Christianity, in Newman's view, is the Incarnation, which he calls the "central aspect of Christianity out of which three main aspects of its teaching take their rise, the sacramental, the hierarchical, and the ascetic." By distinguishing the idea from its form or expression, Newman made it possible for Christian thinkers to hold fast to the idea that the present church is not identical with apostolic Christianity, admitting the developments that took place. Not everything we identify with Christianity need have originated in the apostolic age, as long as the later developments are consistent with the original idea.

2. The central idea of Christianity is an evaluative category that allows Newman to critically deal with growth, change, and development within the tradition. Some developments are genuine; others are not. Chapter five bears

the title "Genuine Developments Contrasted with Corruptions." "The only question that can be raised is whether the said Catholic faith, as now held, is logically, as well as historically the representative of the ancient faith. This then is the subject to which I have as yet addressed myself, and I have maintained that modern Catholicism is nothing else but simply the legitimate growth and complement, that is, the natural and necessary development, of the doctrine of the early church, and that its divine authority is included in the divinity of Christianity."

3. The development of Christianity is modeled on the analogy of organic growth, i.e. the growth of a plant, dog, or fish. We use the analogy of physical growth, wrote Newman, "which is such that the parts and proportions of the developed form, however altered, correspond to those which belong to its rudiments. The adult animal has the same make as it had on its birth; young birds do not grow into fishes, nor does the child degenerate into the brute, wild or domestic. . . ."[13] Echoing Newman and defending his theory, Chesterton quipped, "When we say that a puppy develops into a dog, we do not mean that his growth is a gradual compromise with a cat; we mean that he becomes more doggy and not less."[14]

4. The original seed, following the biological analogy, has within itself all the latent developments that will take place. The unity of the tradition derives from its origins. There is, therefore, an inevitability and necessity to the genuine developments that took place in the Christian past.

5. Only the forms or expressions, not the original idea, change.

Newman has gone beyond the Eusebian view in some notable respects. In the older view, the only progress or growth recognized was the spread of Christianity from one village to another, from one people to another, and the gradual expansion of Christianity and missionizing of the world. Newman proposes a theory that recognizes change at a deeper level, i.e. gradual progress and development in the understanding and comprehension of the original idea. He will not allow, however, that the idea itself changes. What Christianity meant for mankind at its beginning remains the same in every historical epoch. His solution provided a satisfying interpretation of historical change without sacrificing the wholeness, unity, and apostolicity of the Christian faith. The tenacity of Newman's theory among Christian intellectuals of every confessional stripe is a testimony to its success in dealing with the new problems posed by historical thinking. Nevertheless, the residual elements of Eusebianism are still apparent.

In the Eusebian portrait of Christianity, we have singled out several characteristics.

1. Primacy of the apostolic age.

2. Centrality of doctrine as the defining mark of Christianity.

3. A dualistic view of church history, i.e. a history in which true Christianity is set off against false Christianity and the true faith is the standard by which one judges any later form of Christianity.

4. Christianity is, at its beginning and ever after, one system of truth.

Newman's theory conforms to this model on every count except that he has provided a way of explaining the discrepancies between apostolic Christianity and the later forms.


ADOLF VON HARNACK

The problem of historical change did not present itself to Protestants in the same fashion as it did for Roman Catholics. Newman wished to explain how the *church,* specifically the Roman Catholic church in the nineteenth century, could be seen as a logical and historical development of the apostolic faith. Protestants, remembering the debates of the Reformation, sought continuity between apostolic Christianity and their beliefs, not in the church but in the idea of the *gospel.* In modern times, the classical Protestant view found expression in the theory of the Hellenization of the gospel, whose most brilliant exponent was Adolf von Harnack, the great nineteenth-century historian of Christian dogma.

In the winter semester 1899–1900, Harnack gave a series of public lectures at the University of Berlin, where he was professor.[15] The lectures, entitled "The Essence of Christianity," were quickly published and became a runaway best seller in Germany. The book was immediately translated into many languages and read all over the world. By 1927 it had gone through fourteen editions in Germany and as many translations into other languages.

In these lectures, Harnack set forth in simple form the ideas and historical conclusions he had presented at length in the seven volumes of his *History of Dogma,* which he had begun to publish in 1884.

His message was simple: "The gospel entered the world, not as a doctrine but as a joyful message and as a power of the Spirit of God." In the course of the first few centuries in the history of Christianity, this gospel was transformed into the dogmatic and institutional Christianity we know from the history of the church. In the process, the original message of Jesus was obscured. The chief elements of this original faith were, in Harnack's view, the belief in the fatherhood of God, divine providence, the brotherhood of men as God's children, and the infinite value of the individual human person. Originally the gospel was a message *of* Jesus, i.e. a message proclaimed by Jesus about God and man, but the church made this gospel into a message *about* Jesus. Jesus, however, was its "personal realization and its strength and this he is felt to be still."

"The religion of the Gospel is based on . . . [the] belief . . . that . . . by looking to him, this historical person, it becomes certain to the believer that God rules heaven and earth and that God, the Judge, is also Father and Redeemer. The religion of the Gospel is the religion which makes the highest moral demands, the simplest and the most difficult, and discloses the contradiction in which every man finds himself towards them. But it also procures redemption from such misery, by drawing the life of men into the inexhaustible and blessed life of Jesus

Christ, who has overcome the world and called sinners to himself."[16]

Harnack believed that Christianity began as a movement within Judaism that proclaimed this joyous message to mankind. At a very early date, however, new forces entered the life of the church from the surrounding world and began what eventually became a transformation of this original gospel into dogmatic Christianity. Dogma was not part of the original faith, but a later development. "Dogmatic Christianity is therefore a definite stage in the history of the development of Christianity. It corresponds to the ancient mode of thought, but has nevertheless continued to a very great extent in the following epochs, though subject to great transformations. . . ." Dogma, then, "in its conception and development is a work of the Greek spirit on the soil of the Gospel." In his construction of the past, Harnack distinguished an early period, before dogmatic Christianity took root, followed by a long period in which dogma grew and developed within the bosom of the church. As a historian he sets forth two tasks in his history of dogma: 1. to ascertain the origin of dogma as a form of Christian thinking, and 2. to describe the development of dogma, i.e. the variations that mark its history.[17]

Some criticized Harnack for simply identifying dogma with Greek philosophy, but he was himself quite careful to insist that dogma was a work of the Greek spirit "on the soil of the Gospel." It was the original Christian message that provided the soil out of which dogma grew. Dogma is a development *within* the Christian tradition.

"The foolishness of identifying dogma and Greek philosophy never entered my mind; on the contrary, the peculiarity of ecclesiastical dogma seemed to me to lie in the very fact that, on the one hand, it gave expression to Christian Monotheism and the central significance of the person of Christ, and, on the other hand, comprehended this religious faith and the historical knowledge connected with it in a philosophic system."[18] Harnack's theory of the Hellenization of the gospel is an attempt to explain why it is that the *Christian religion* took the form it did in the course of its history.

The plausibility of this interpretation of the Christian past—and its almost universal acceptance in Protestant circles, and more recently its attraction to Catholic thinkers—arises from the obvious fact that the Christianity of Justin Martyr in the middle of the second century, or Clement of Alexandria at the end of the second century, or Origen in the middle of the third century, is quite unlike that of Mark or Paul in the first century, or the preaching of Jesus. Some differences noted by Harnack are the following: the development of fixed offices such as that of the bishop as channels of God's grace and signs of authority in the church; the conviction that the relation of the individual to God and Christ is dependent on the acceptance of an inspired book and a divinely attested rule of faith; the belief that a visible earthly community is the people of the new covenant; the belief that faith is not simply trust in God but also intellectual assent to a body of doctrine.

Harnack dates the beginning of these developments

toward the end of the first century, but it was not until the third century that the Hellenic influences came to dominate the Christian consciousness and to permeate Christian institutions. "The most decisive division, therefore, falls before the end of the first century; or more correctly, the relatively new element, the Greek, which is of importance for the forming of the Church as a commonwealth, and consequently for the formation of its doctrine, is clearly present in the churches even in the Apostolic age. Two hundred years, however, passed before it made itself completely at home in the Gospel, although there were points of connection inherent in the Gospel."[19]

The theory of the Hellenization of the gospel did not originate with Harnack, but his *History of Dogma* has had such enormous influence on Christian thinking that Hellenization is usually associated with his name. Actually his theory fits in remarkably well with the older Reformation conception of church history.[20] Harnack's achievement was to bring the insights of the reformers to a new expression by filtering them through the new historical consciousness of the nineteenth century and giving them a sound historical grounding. The reformers had been critical of many abuses of medieval Christendom, especially of practices that subordinated God's grace to man's works, but they were not critical of the traditional dogmas of the Trinity or Christology, nor were they critical of the idea of dogma itself. They affirmed their belief in the decisions of the ancient councils.

Nevertheless, the similarity between Harnack's views and those of the reformers is greater than the dissimilarities. The reformers did not talk about the fatherhood of God and the brotherhood of man, as did Harnack, but they made the idea of the gospel the standard for judging the history of Christianity. Harnack, too, believed that the earliest form of the gospel was the definitive statement of the eternal meaning of the Christian faith and that this gospel could serve as a critical principle for interpreting any later developments within Christianity. "As far as possible, the course of development is to be judged by the Gospel in its original form. . . ."[21] Harnack is much more aware than his predecessors, however, that as a historian he cannot simply use the "gospel" as his critical principle. In fact there are two ways of critically evaluating the history of dogma: 1. the historical conditions of the times and the consequences of the historical development, and 2. the gospel.[22] Harnack used both in his historical work, though his sympathy lies more with the latter than with the former.

There was only one gospel, and it remained the same from generation to generation. Or at least it should remain the same. If the gospel changed in every age, it could never serve as the one standard to interpret the whole of Christian history. Some things remain the same, while others are always changing. The "essence" of Christianity always transcends every historical expression, even though some expressions are more-faithful embodiments of this essence than others. The "essence of Christianity" is itself not historical, and Harnack never presents the essence itself as a historical phenomenon. Though speaks a great deal about the changes and developments within the history of Christianity, the Christian religion, his term for the religion of Jesus, itself does not change and develop. Christianity does not *become* anything in the course of its history. For example, he insists as we have seen, that it is Christianity that gave rise to dogma—dogma is not simply Greek philosophy—but he does not draw any inferences from this conclusion. If the Christian religion engendered dogma, what does this tell us about Christianity? Instead Harnack sees developments within Christianity either as corruptions or deviations of the original faith or external changes that do not affect the heart of the faith. What Christianity *becomes* does not shed any light on what Christianity *is*. What it *is* is defined by what it was at the beginning.

### THE THEORY OF "EARLY CATHOLICISM"

In present historical and theological circles the Harnackian notion of Hellenization has given way to a new theory called "early Catholicism." Further historical study of early Christianity has shown that "Hellenization" began at a somewhat earlier date than Harnack thought, and scholars have devised a modified form at Harnack's theory to fit their new historical information. The basic historical construction of early Christianity, however, is quite parallel to that of Harnack. Further, most of the scholars who speak of "early Catholicism" are Protestants who have been influenced by the ideas of the reformers.

Early Catholicism, writes John Elliott, is "a term used to designate characteristics which the primitive Christian community has in common with the catholic church of the late second and following centuries."[23] Some of the features of early catholicism, according to Elliott, are the following: organization of the church according to a hierarchal pattern; the bishop as the chief authority within the Christian communities; a strictly formulated rule of faith to which all members of the community must be obedient; decline of the place of Christ's redemptive work in favor of an increased emphasis on moralism; development of the idea of apostolic succession and authority transmitted from one bishop to another; an authoritarian interpretation of the Scriptures binding on all; excessive emphasis on sacraments; collection of the writings of the primitive church into a fixed book which becomes the standard for all matters of faith and life.

It is clear from this list that many of the marks of "early catholicism" are the same that Harnack considered to be marks of emerging dogmatic and ecclesiastical Christianity. The chief difference between the present theory and that of Harnack is that present-day scholars who speak of early catholicism are largely New Testament specialists, whereas Harnack was a historian of Christianity. This means that "early catholicism" is an interpretative key for understanding the New Testament, whereas Harnack was interested in the whole historical development of Christianity. According to the present view, books that contain "early catholic" elements are Luke, sections of Matthew, the pastoral epistles (I and II Timothy, Titus), Ephesians, Jude, 2 Peter, and, outside the New Testament, I Clement, the epistles of Ignatius of

Antioch, and others. "Early catholicism" is a *historical* period in the history of Christianity, extending roughly from the eighth decade of the first century to the middle of the second century. It follows on the first historical period in the church's history, i.e. the years from A.D. 30 to A.D. 70–80. The chief witnesses to the earlier period are the writings of St. Paul and the traditions embedded in the earlier strata of the gospels. At times, one has the feeling that "early catholicism" is almost identical with non-Pauline Christianity.

We can illustrate the use of "early catholicism" as a historical category by reference to an essay by Ernst Kaesemann entitled "Ministry and Community in the New Testament." In this essay, Kaesemann discusses the relation between the ministerial office and the early Christian community as it developed within the primitive Christian church. The bulk of the essay focuses on Paul's understanding of the ministry in relation to his conception of *charisma*, i.e. the gifts bestowed on Christians through the grace of God. Kaesemann's argument is that in Paul's view the whole of life stands under the gift of charisma and that Paul's understanding of ministry derives from this gift. The new life bestowed by the gift of charisma is, in Kaesemann's view, intelligible only in light of Paul's doctrine of justification by faith. God makes impious men righteous by his grace (*justificatio impii*); he gives life to the dead and sets up his kingdom where demonic powers have held sway. "Paul's doctrine of the charismata," writes Kaesemann, "is to be understood as the projection into ecclesiology [doctrine of the church] of the doctrine of justification by faith. . . ."[24]

Because these graces, or *charismata,* are given to all Christians, Paul does not set off the community of all Christians from a distinct office, i.e. the ministry, in the church. The many "offices," i.e. services of the individual Christians, flow out of this gift of grace. In this situation, where "all Christians are regarded as endowed with charisma," there is no mention of ideas of "sacred space, sacred time, the right of representative action in the cultus [e.g. a priest acting for the congregation], of sacred persons in the sense of both Judaism and the pagan religions," i.e. no special privileged group or class. In Paul's understanding, "All the baptized are 'office bearers.'" Thus Paul does not establish fixed offices or institutions, ranks and dignities; authority rests only in the concrete act of ministry as this flows from the charismata given by God.[25]

Kaesemann believes that this understanding of office and ministry was characteristic of the very primitive church but that, very shortly after Paul, a quite different conception began to emerge: "It would not be practical for us to extend this investigation of the relation between office and community over the whole of the New Testament. But it is nevertheless useful to sketch in bold outline, and as a kind of foil to the Pauline outlook, that antithesis of it which has gained a foothold in the New Testament itself, especially in the Pastorals and in Luke's writings." In these somewhat later writings, the pastorals even being attributed to Paul, we discover for the first time the development of an office that stands over against the community, and this office is the true bearer of the Spirit; the idea of an apostolic delegate who was the representative and spokesman for the whole community; the idea of a succession of authoritative teachers and leaders; a distinction between clergy and laymen. These developments contravene the ideas of Paul and begin to forge quite a new understanding of the Christian church.

Commenting on I Tim. 6:20, "O Timothy, guard what has been entrusted to you. . . ." Kaesemann writes, "The significance of this is that an office which stands over against the rest of the community is now the real bearer of the Spirit; and the primitive Christian view, that every Christian receives the Spirit in his baptism, recedes into the background and indeed, for all practical purposes, disappears. It is equally clear that this state of affairs cannot be reconciled with the Pauline doctrine of the *charismata*. The Jewish heritage expels the Pauline, in at least one central area of the Christian proclamation."

As proof of his theory, Kaesemann cites I Tim. 4:14 and II Tim. 1:6. "Do not neglect the gift [*charisma*] you have, which was given you by prophetic utterance when the elders laid their hands upon you." (I Tim. 4:14) In this passage the gift, or *charisma,* refers not to the grace given all Christians, but to the special office of the ministry received through the laying on of hands, i.e. to ordination. This shift in understanding from the earlier Pauline idea, Kaesemann interprets as a mark of the "transition to early catholicism."[26]

Kaesemann is too careful a scholar and historian to

overlook the historical reasons for the development to
early catholicism. He traces, for example, some of the new
ideas to the influence of Judaism; others he sees as the
result of new circumstances. "We cannot overlook the fact
that need and necessity were the godparents of this transformation and we shall therefore be guarded in our criticism of its rightness." As the early Christian communities
grew and expanded, some adjustment to the new situation
would be necessary. Nevertheless Kaesemann believes
that these developments did not have to take the form
that they did, and that from a theological point of view
they cannot be justified. "What makes the whole process
so questionable theologically (from a Pauline standpoint,
at any rate), and indeed marks the transition to early
catholicism, is that the change is associated with and
founded on, not need and historical necessity but a the-
oretical principle of tradition and legitimate succession;
so that, in effect, the Spirit is made to appear as the organ
and rationale of a theory."[27]

Kaesemann adds the parenthetical remark "from a
Pauline standpoint" to explain his criticism of this new
development, but it is apparent from the spirit as well
as the explicit argument of the essay that "Pauline" is
equivalent to authentically Christian. Elsewhere in the
essay he contrasts other sections of the New Testament,
especially Acts, with the Pauline viewpoint. He criticizes
Luke's ideas of "tradition and legitimate succession" as
marks of the advent of early catholicism. In Kaesemann's
view the Pauline doctrine of *charisma* was lost in the following generations, and even in later Christian history, in-

cluding the time of the Reformation, no one saw clearly the implications of Paul's views. The reformers did not abolish the ordained ministry, and Kaesemann wonders why Protestantism "has never made a serious attempt to create a Church order which reflected the Pauline doctrine of charisma but has left this to the sects."[28]

It is not surprising that some Roman Catholic scholars have found Kaesemann's arguments less than convincing. They see them as little more than a restatement of the classical themes of the Reformation and an attempt to read these ideas back into the primitive church. Kaesemann himself admits that the Pauline doctrine of *charisma* is simply another form of justification by grace through faith. "On what grounds does Kaesemann claim that his selection from the New Testament specifically constitute the 'gospel'?" asks Hans Küng. Why should Paul be set up as the standard for the rest of the New Testament or the later history of the church? "Can Kaesemann base himself on anything more than on an a priori Protestant viewpoint?"[29] Kaesemann is in fact proposing a canon within the canon of the New Testament, and the distinctive marks of this canon arise out of the Protestant Reformation. He is faithful to the intention of the reformers by formulating a theological principle for the interpretation of early Christianity that has its origin in Luther.

Harnack's theory of the Hellenization of the gospel, and the current idea of early catholicism, are variants of a common historical construction of the past. Both are sophisticated modern forms of the Eusebian view of history.

1. Hellenization and early catholicism are historical

categories that serve to set off the earliest period in the history of Christianity from the entire later history.

2. Implicitly, and in some cases explicitly, the earlier period is thought to be normative for the later history. Early catholicism and Hellenization describe a time in the history of the church when the original Christian faith was undergoing a transmutation into something inferior to what it had been at the beginning.

3. These theories view the history of the church in "dualistic" terms. That is, they set up an idea of "true" Christianity and use it to interpret various "false" forms of Christianity that developed in the course of history. They assume that Protestantism is the most authentic expression of apostolic Christianity. The term "catholicism" itself suggests that when these historians speak about *early* Catholicism they have in mind a form of Christianity resembling Roman Catholicism. Why should the beginning of a transformation of the original faith be called "catholicizing"? Indeed, the characteristics of early catholicism are quite similar to the perversions that the reformers sought to reform in the church of the sixteenth century: emphasis on works rather than grace, faith as belief in a body of revealed truth rather than trust in God's grace, apostolic succession of bishops as the source of authority in the church, etc.

4. True Christianity is identified with a single central idea, e.g. Harnack's gospel or Kaesemann's justification by faith. This idea remains for all times the distinctive mark of true Christianity.

ARE THE CRITICS CRITICAL ENOUGH?

Most New Testament scholars and historians of early Christianity consider themselves to be highly critical in their dealing with the New Testament writings. By the standards of past scholarship and the facile assumptions of many Christians, these scholars are indeed critical. My argument is that they are not critical enough, and that they have not examined their own assumptions carefully. By their historical construction of early Christianity, they perpetuate the idea that Christianity can be understood by reference to the time of origins, and that the time of origins is the standard by which one measures any later form or expression of Christianity. If one reads through studies of the New Testament, one gets the definite impression that New Testament scholars believe that once one has shown how an idea or belief came to be part of the New Testament and what it means in the New Testament, that the historical task has been completed. New Testament monographs may go back five hundred years in Jewish history to explain a text or an idea found in the New Testament, but they seldom go even fifty years into the history of the text or idea after the New Testament.

Historical understanding is first and foremost an attempt to set any given phenomenon within its context. What were the forces at work on a given thinker; what is the background of a certain idea; how do social and political conditions affect the development of a new institution? The placing of past phenomena into context requires, however, that we look not only at the things that went *before,* but also the things that happened after. Is not the development of the ideas and beliefs of primitive Christianity *after* they have become part of the earliest tradition as significant as their history before that time? By the time the New Testament took the form we know today, Christianity was just beginning its historical development. One could reply: But the study of the later history is the task of the church historian. This, however, misses the point. The reason why there is a distinction between New Testament study and church history as separate disciplines is due to the view of origins forged by the Eusebian construction of the past. There is no basis within the historical material of the first several centuries of Christianity to suggest a division between New Testament and church history. Even though most scholars today would reject the traditional idea of biblical authority, the very division of labor between church historians and New Testament scholars indicates that remnants of the older idea still linger on. What comes later may be historically interesting and important, but it is not thought to be *theologically* significant. That is, later developments do not contribute to an understanding of what Christianity really is or should be. What it really is can be learned only from the earliest period.

We cannot discover what Christianity "is" by an exegesis of the biblical texts or by uncovering the earliest strata of the Christian tradition. The Christian movement can be understood only in light of its historical development, i.e. what it *became* within the course of its history. The New Testament has a *future* as well as a past. What *becomes* of a historical phenomenon is as much a statement of what it is as what it was at the beginning. The religion of Jesus did *become* the dogmatic and ecclesiastical Christianity, and the charismatic ministry of Paul did *develop* into the organized ministry of the second and third centuries. Primitive Christianity is the first stage in the history of the Christian church. The events and ideas of this period yield no ultimate norm as to what Christianity *really* is or should be.

The passage of time is irreversible. Every moment, every day, every week, every year is unique and unrepeatable. Christians who have been interested in the reform of the church—whether in organization, in thought, or in its mores—have consistently appealed to the past, and specifically to the most ancient past, to justify their reform efforts. The appeal to origins has great persuasive power, but as compelling as it may be, it loses its credibility when one takes seriously the historical character of Christianity. For example, today some say that the liturgy should take the shape of a meal, not a sacrificial ritual; that the priest should celebrate the liturgy facing the people, not with his back to them; that the Eucharist should be a joyful eschatological meal, not a somber penitential service; *because* this is the way early Christians celebrated the liturgy. But these visions of the past—though they have power to stir the hearts of men—cannot tell us what we should do today. If we believe we can restore apostolic practices, or reproduce Paul's teaching on grace and faith, or remodel our ministry on the primitive pattern, we delude ourselves; the past is past, and when we attempt to restore the past we always create something new—not necessarily something better—which was not there before.

The circular clock is seductive. We see the hands go around and around as though each hour and day were part of an eternal merry-go-round. If we believe that time is linear, perhaps our timepieces should also be linear devices. How deceptive to speak of "setting back" the clock. Time never runs backward. Every moment is unique, and has its unique place on the clock of history. We cannot take a moment from the past and place it somewhere else on the historical spectrum. We can only remember the past, not relive or restore it. Some moments stand out as singular, but even these cannot leap over the times that intervene. The Christian movement began at a particular moment in history, but its meaning, its significance, was not given once, nor was it ever captured by one age or idea. Indeed its meaning is still unfolding as long as new moments continue to appear and the future stretches before us. Now we know in part, as we see through a glass darkly.

## CHAPTER VII

# *You Can't Go Home Again*

THE apostolic age is a creation of the Christian imagination. There never was a Golden Age when the church was whole, perfect, pure—virginal. The faith was not purer, the Christians were not braver, the church was not one and undivided. Like any new and charismatic movement—Black Muslims under Malcolm X, Pentecostalism in our day—the early Christian communities could and did make rigorous demands on their adherents, enthusiasm abounded, and their dreams seemed closer to realization. Yet these are common experiences of beginnings; Christianity is not unique in the ardor of its first converts. The very early history of Christianity appears ideal to later generations, just as anything new seems more perfect—a new marriage, friendship, apartment, job, club, or automobile. The problems attendant on growth, success, increased numbers, acceptance, even prestige, do not present themselves to new movements at the very beginning. It may take five or ten years or a generation for them to appear.

The distinguishing mark of the first Christian generation is that it is the first generation. It is not the wholeness, perfection, or completeness that impresses the historian of early Christianity. Rather, it is the incompleteness, openness, and newness that strike us. The bishop's metaphor was virginity—a symbol of perfection to the mind of a fourth-century Christian. Perhaps we can rescue the metaphor for our day by suggesting that virginity implies incompleteness.

Eusebius thought it was better to be a virgin, and lamented the church's loss; we might say it is better not to be a virgin: losing one's virginity is a stage in life's way. Since Christianity is a historical movement, its meaning and significance cannot be seen in the past thirty years. Early Christianity yearned for fulfillment, for it longed to uncover new worlds and it sought opportunities for testing. What the Christian movement *is* would not be revealed until later. Its destiny is not apparent at the beginning. The myth of the apostolic age gave later Christians the conviction that everything significant was to be found at the beginning. Revelation was thought to have ceased with the last apostle. The meager sources from the first generation, and the paucity of historical knowledge, gave the Christian imagination ample space to roam. Left to its own devisings, the Christian mind could and did find everything it later identified with Christianity in the earliest period.

The Christian intellect is no longer left to its own musings. It has been tempered by the fire of critical historical reason. In this chapter I wish to show how historical reason has altered our view of the apostolic age.

The argument can be summarized under two points:

1. Christianity does not begin with any one idea about the meaning and significance of Jesus. 2. What we call the apostolic writings, i.e. the New Testament, and the chief testimony from the early history of Christianity, are not the first form or expression of the Christian faith. Rather, these writings, though they incorporate some of the earliest material we have, are only representatives of various stages of the development of early Christian tradition. The New Testament represents a "random" selection from the Christian tradition as it had developed by the end of the first one or two generations.

## CHRISTIANITY AN INNOVATION

The Christian religion began as an innovation within Judaism. The vision of Jesus of Nazareth, though rooted in the experience of the Jewish people and dependent on the Jewish tradition, was not the same as that of his Jewish contemporaries. If Jesus were judged by the standard of the received tradition, he would have been, and was, considered a rebel and radical who overthrew the traditions of the fathers. His preaching and his view of his own mission, while understandable in light of the Jewish tradition, were new and different. Likewise, the vision of the first Christians arose out of the experience they had with Jesus, but it was not the same as that of Jesus himself.

For example, the Kingdom of God, so central to the preaching of Jesus, is hardly mentioned in the writings of Paul. The preaching of the apostles included a message about Jesus himself, whereas Jesus spoke little about himself, but a great deal about the coming of God's Kingdom. The Apostles saw Jesus differently from the way Jesus saw himself, not simply because they were not Jesus and had a different perspective, but because they looked back on his death and Resurrection and made of these events the center of their preaching.

Somewhat later, another generation of Christians, who learned that the end of the world might not come as soon as they expected, created yet another vision. They did not live in anticipation of an immediate end, but realized that they might live out their lives till their deaths. Yet they included in their conception of Christianity the experience of the earlier apostles and the preaching of Jesus. They, too, were innovators who revised and reinterpreted the tradition they received.

### WHAT WAS THE ORIGINAL FAITH?

What, then, was the original Christian faith? Over the past 150 years, Christian scholars have launched an intensive critical examination of the sacred documents of Christianity—the most thorough study ever attempted on any major religious movement. Men have always studied the sacred documents of their various faiths—for edification, nurture, instruction, comfort—but up until modern times, this study has been motivated less by critical and more by religious considerations.

In modern times, Christian scholars—not hostile critics or foes of Christianity—adapted the tools of historical critical science to the data of early Christianity. In this light, the New Testament was viewed not as the authoritative source of Christian faith, but as a collection of historical sources to be compared, contrasted, and interpreted in light of the other literature from the period. Christians began to view the New Testament not simply as an inspired book given by God—in light of its divine origin—but as a historical document from the ancient world.[1]

The New Testament writings reflect the experience and practice of Christians over a period of more than one hundred years and in various cultural and ecclesiastical settings. Within the New Testament there are books written during the first thirty years after the death of Jesus, i.e. A.D. 50–60, and there are others written seventy to one hundred years after his death. Some of the New Testament writings reflect a very early stage in Christian thinking, when men expected the Lord to return before their deaths; others represent attitudes that assume Christianity is here to stay for the duration, and reflect Christian communities eager to accommodate to the prevailing cultural and ethical values.

Once we tended to look at early Christian literature in two stages: 1. New Testament writings (apostolic age), and 2. Apostolic Fathers (turn of second century). Now we know that this is a false distinction both on chronological and theological grounds. Some of the writings of the apostolic fathers are contemporaneous with or earlier than certain New Testament writings, and the beliefs and attitudes of certain New Testament authors are closer to Ignatius or I Clement than they are to Paul or Mark. The Acts of the Apostles and the pastoral epistles are contemporaneous with I Clement, and 2 Peter is probably later than all these. The Didache, on the other hand, is probably earlier than Acts or the Gospel of John.[2] Which of these writings are to be considered authentic witnesses to the original Christian faith?

Not only do the New Testament writings arise in different historical situations and different chronological periods; they also incorporate many divergent elements whose original meaning and intention may be quite different from the meaning given them in their present form in the New Testament. Even a casual reading of the Gospels turns up much parallel material, obviously from common sources, but frequently used and interpreted in quite different ways. Luke presents the parable of the wedding feast in such a way that it encourages the mission of the church to extend itself to all men; Matthew presents the same parable as a statement of the rigorous demands made upon anyone who joins the Christian community. "Go into the highways and byways," says Luke; Matthew concludes with the tale of the man who was thrown out of the banquet because he did not have the wedding garment: "Many are called, but few are chosen."

Christians did not everywhere and in all places believe the same things about Jesus and his message, about Judaism, the church, the Spirit, even during, indeed especially during, the first three decades of the church's history. Diversity of belief and practice existed from the beginning.[3] If we look at the picture of Christianity given us by Paul, Matthew, or John, we see at once that from the beginning, in A.D. 30–35, to their times enormous changes have al-

ready occurred. John, writing at the end of the first century, is as far from the beginning of Christianity as we
are from the presidency of Theodore Roosevelt!

We can illustrate some of these changes by the terms
early Christians used to refer to Jesus. Jesus, who spoke
little of himself, would not have used terms such as Messiah, Son of man, Lord, Son of God, and others to refer
to himself. The early Christians, however, did use these
and other terms, though not all at once. The earliest
traditions show that a development took place from the
time immediately after the Resurrection and continued
through the first century—more precisely, for the first four
hundred years of Christian history. Indeed, it continues
to this day. But there is a hardening of the tradition toward
the end of the first century, and the earliest history of
Christological times can be uncovered by a careful study
of the Gospels.[4]

### THE EARLIEST TESTIMONIES

Jesus came proclaiming the Kingdom of God. To the
small band of Jews who lived and traveled with Jesus, his
crucifixion came as a great disappointment, and though
his Resurrection renewed their confidence in the rightness
of his cause, they had no clear idea what these strange
events meant. Who was this Jesus? The earliest testimonies to Jesus arise out of the charismatic and enthusi-
astic religious fervor provoked by the Resurrection. Events
were moving fast, and Jesus' followers did their thinking
on the run—or more accurately, while doing other things.

Early Christian beliefs do not arise out of theological en-
claves; they were formed in disputes between Christians
and their adversaries, in the setting of a cultic meal, while
explaining their convictions to a new convert, or in the
telling of tales about Jesus to the young. Christian beliefs
grew out of the situations in life (*Sitz im Leben*) in
which early Christians regularly found themselves.

There were no set beliefs agreed on by all; nor were
there any ground rules on how to determine what to say
or think or do; nor was there any acknowledged authority
for deciding such question. Let us suppose that in the
year A.D. 35 two men, Michael and Ephraim, became
Christians in Jerusalem; Michael went to the town of
Edessa in Syria to live, and Ephraim went to Alexandria
in Egypt. On arrival in their respective cities, each told
others about the remarkable man Jesus. After telling their
friends about Jesus, let us say Michael and Ephraim organized Christian congregations. Almost immediately,
problems would arise. What should we do about the Jewish
law? What should we do when we gather for worship? How
are we to understand the meaning of this passage from
the Jewish Scriptures? What was it Jesus was supposed
to have said on this question? The questions were endless,
and the Christians in Edessa and the Christians in Alexandria would not answer all in the same way—the traditions Michael and Ephraim brought with them were too
embryonic, too undefined, to answer every new question
or settle every dispute. They had to make up their own
minds as they understood their own situation and the memories they brought with them.

Now let us change the scene to A.D. 75. Forty years have passed. In the meantime the Jews have been defeated by the Romans, and Jerusalem has been destroyed. Also, the Christian movement has spread widely and solidified its traditions. Let us now suppose that someone from Edessa travels to Alexandria and learns that there is a Christian community there. He seeks it out and finally is able to spend several days with his fellow Christians. To his surprise, he learns that they have little in common except a common loyalty to Jesus, and the fragments of his words that have been handed on orally. And even the fragments of his sayings are not in quite the form they are in Edessa. The visitor from Edessa discovers that the Christians in Alexandria do not keep the Jewish law, whereas his congregation keeps it exactly, admitting no one to the Christian community without circumcision. The Alexandrians pray to Jesus, whereas in Edessa all prayers are addressed solely to God the Father, and in Alexandria they believe that the resurrection of all men referred not to the end of time, but to the new life in Baptism, whereas the Christians in Edessa think this is a denial of the final resurrection. Both are shocked at the practices and beliefs of the others. Who is the representative of the original faith?

## THE "SON OF MAN"

The above is hypothetical, though the examples are taken from actual historical sources. The same phenomenon can be seen in the use of the term "Son of man" in the Synoptic Gospels.[5] In Luke 12:8–9 Jesus says, "And I tell you, everyone who acknowledges me before men, the Son of man also will acknowledge before the angels of God; but he who denies me before men will be denied before the angels of God." In this saying—perhaps from the lips of Jesus—the Son of man is someone other than Jesus. Jesus refers to the Son of man in the third person. Further, the "work" of the Son of man is thought to take place at some future date, i.e. at the judgment at the end of time. Very early in the Christian tradition, the term Son of man was identified with Jesus because of the Resurrection, and was understood to refer to something Jesus would do in the immediate future or present: "The Son of man came to seek and to save the lost"; or "The Son of man came not to be served by to serve and to give his life as a ransom for many." As this last statement suggests, it was also adapted to fit the death and Resurrection of Jesus—ideas quite foreign to the pre-Christian Jewish use of the term. "Behold, we are going up to Jerusalem; and the Son of man will be delivered to the chief priests and scribes, and they will condemn him to death and deliver him to the Gentiles; and they will mock him, and spit upon him, and scourge him, and kill him; after three days he will rise."

The sayings about the Son of man are part of the earliest stratum of Christological formulations, but even these are part of a process of development stretching over a number of years and in different early-Christian communities. Note that these sayings make the initial step of attempting to interpret Jesus' life and preaching in light

of his death and Resurrection, but note also that they really
say little about who Jesus was, where he had come from,
why he was able to do what he did, what his relation to
God was. But the early Christians wanted to say more, and
the situations in the life of the community required them
to define further who this Jesus was. (Obviously, this
whole process of formulation took place with little reflection; as new situations arose and old ones recurred, terms,
ideas, and phrases found their way into the various traditions and became the vehicles for expressing what the
communities had experienced in their lives.)

A second stratum, still Jewish but now overlaid with
Hellenistic concepts, called Jesus the Lord (Kyrios), the
Messiah, and Son of David. Because of the political over-
tones of the term Messiah (Christ), Jesus had preferred
not to let himself be called Messiah. Nevertheless, this
term has some similarities with Son of man and Christians
began to use it for Jesus. In Mark 14:61–62 these words
are ascribed to Jesus: " 'Are you the Christ, the Son of the
Blessed?' And Jesus said, 'I am; and you will see the Son
of man sitting at the right hand of Power, and coming with
the clouds of heaven.' " Here the term Christ refers to
something in the future; elsewhere it is used of Jesus'
present ministry. In answer to the question of John's disciples "Who are you?" Jesus replies, "Go and tell John
what you hear and see; the blind receive their sight and
the lame walk, lepers are cleansed and the deaf hear, and
the dead are raised up and the poor have good news
preached to them."

In a later stratum[6] of the tradition, we meet for the

first time the idea that Jesus was "sent" from heaven, and that after his Resurrection he reigns as Lord until the end of time. But the greatest "innovation" in Christological thinking before the formation of the New Testament itself is the introduction of the idea that Jesus existed as a heavenly being before his birth, i.e. that he was pre-existent and dwelt with God. Clearly the next step would be to call him God or at least God's Son. Once the idea of pre-existence was established in the tradition, Jesus' birth took on new significance. Now his birth was not simply the beginning of the life of an extraordinary man; his birth was an "incarnation," i.e. the moment when a divine being took on human flesh. "In the beginning was the Word, and the Word was with God, and the Word was God. . . . And the Word became flesh and dwelt among us, full of grace and truth; we have beheld his glory, glory as of the only Son from the Father." (John 1) And in Paul: ". . . Christ Jesus, who, though he was in the form of God, did not count equality with God a thing to be grasped, but emptied himself, taking the form of a servant, being born in the likeness of men." (Philippians 2) Let us suppose our friend from Edessa brought with him a "Son of man" Christology to Alexandria and discovered there that Jesus was revered as a pre-existent divine being, the Son of God. Who would have the greater claim on Christian truth? The "Son of man" Christology would be earlier, but would it do justice to the fullness men had come to know in Jesus?

If we might take some liberty with the metaphor of "returning home," we could say, "You can't go home

again," because there is no home to go to. It is not that
the home has changed or that the person returning home
is no longer the same—though these also are true—but
that early Christianity never settled down long enough to
make a home. There never was an "original Christian
faith" or a "native Christian language." The further back
one searches, the more unformed the tradition becomes.
There is no moment or man or age or idea to which we
can return and say: that is the Christian thing. The Christian phenomenon can only be grasped by looking at the
historical experience of Christianity as it stretches from
its beginning to the present and into the future. And because the Christian movement is still very much alive,
we do not know what its final destiny will be. In future years it may become something even we have trouble
recognizing. Historically, it is absurd to take the first stage
of Christian tradition as definitive for the whole history.
Not only can we not locate precisely what the first stage
was, but even if we could, we would find it so unformed
and embryonic that it could hardly do justice to the reality
of Christianity as we know it from later history. Are the
first words of Neil Armstrong on the moon an adequate
statement of the meaning of the event?

## THE VALUE OF THE NEW TESTAMENT WITNESS

Why should we elevate the apostles above later Christians? Hegel once quipped, "The apostles were not like the
disciples of Socrates, men with other interests, but socially and politically isolated Jews. Christianity had to

begin as the creed of a sect, and there is no Socratic toler-
ance in the zeal of a proselytizing sect."[7] Perhaps this over-
states the case, but not by much. The earliest Christians had
no idea of what Christianity was to become in the centuries to follow. Their experience and their vision were
limited by their own time and situation, just as later Christians also had their limitations. The value of the New
Testament witness is not that it definitely states the truth
about Christianity, but that it bears witness to the earliest
experience of Christianity that we possess. The New
Testament is important because it bears witness to the
unique experiences of the first century, just as the Nicene
Creed bears witness to the unique experiences of the
fourth century, scholastic theology to the Middle Ages,
and historical thinking to the modern period. Its contribution does not lie in any timeless statement of Christian
truth, but in the very time-conditioned expression arising
out of a particular moment in the past.

Each new generation of Christians has at once built on
what it has received from the past, and changed, altered,
reshaped, and added to this inheritance. Perhaps we should
simply invert the historical construction of the Christian
past. Instead of looking primarily to the first period to see
what Christianity is, why not look at the latest experiences
and the events of centuries that lead up to the present.
The earliest testimonies had access to Jesus in a way un-
available to later generations, but later generations had the
advantage of seeing more clearly what Jesus' significance
would be among men.

To illustrate: If we were to rely solely on the earliest

testimonies of Christians, we would have to admit that at
the beginning Christians thought the message of Jesus and
about Jesus was for Jews alone. Very early, some questioned this view, because others, who were non-Jews,
wished to become Christians. The idea of non-Jewish
Christians offended some, but the "innovation" carried the
day and became fundamental to the Christian self-
understanding. Yet, if we were to be faithful to the earliest
tradition, we would have to limit the Christian message to
Jews. Who is prepared to be so fundamentalist about the
past? Here, as in the whole history of Christianity, the
demands of the present and expectation for the future
reshape and reinterpret the received tradition.

LESSONS FROM THE OLD TESTAMENT

Ancient Israel, whose literature extends over many hun-
dreds of years, has given us numerous examples of how
traditions from the past constantly take on new meaning
as they are filtered through new experiences. Gerhard von
Rad, whose Old Testament theology is a study in the history of the reinterpretation of religious tradition, writes:

"Each generation was faced with the ever-identical yet
ever-new task of understanding itself as Israel. In a certain sense, every generation had first to become Israel. Of
course, as a rule the sons were able to recognize themselves in the picture handed on to them by the fathers. But
still this did not exempt each generation from the task of
comprehending itself in faith as the Israel of its own day.
. . . However, in this process of actualization the tradition

here and there had to be reshaped. Theological demands altered—thus, for example, the Elohist's idea of the saving history was brought in alongside the earlier one of the Jahwist. Later ages wanted to understand the theological meaning of more extensive ranges in the history. To satisfy their needs the Deuteronomistic school in the Exile wove into the older complexes its own interpretative interpolations which serve as a framework, and so on. In this way the capital of tradition slowly mounted up—new parts were added, old parts were interpreted. . . . No generation produced a perfectly independent and finished historical work—each continued to work upon what had been handed down to it, the Elohist working upon the Jahwist, the Deuteronomist upon copious older material, while the Chronicler in turn built further upon the foundation of the Deuteronomist."[8]

In the course of centuries, traditions that had once been unified became separated, and others, once disparate, become unified into a new synthesis. In the process, the original, or earliest, meaning was often forgotten, and the new meaning, foreign to the original intention of the authors, took its place. Jeremiah, for example, took the years in the wilderness as a time when Israel's relation to its God, Jahweh, was the purest (Jeremiah 2:2 ff.); Ezekiel, writing in a different setting to a different audience, takes the same experience in the wilderness as a time of disobedience. Isaiah took a traditional oracle (18:1-6) to mean a judgment on the Egyptians, whereas a later editor of the book of Isaiah turns the oracle into a blessing—gifts are brought to the Egyptians (v. 7).

The prophets did not speak in a vacuum. What they wrote was bound to the tradition they inherited—if not, they could hardly identify with and speak to the Jews— and their dependence on the tradition legitimated their message. But they went beyond the tradition and gave it new meaning, new content, and application to new situations. Isaiah takes over ancient traditions about David, but instead of treating them in traditional fashion he makes them apply to the whole of Israel, not to David alone. Israel is to become the sovereign ruler of the people. "In thus 'democratizing' the tradition, Deutero-Isaiah actually robbed it of its specific content. Indeed, the Messianic hope had no place in his prophetic ideas. This bold reshaping of the old David tradition is an example, though admittedly an extreme one, of the freedom with which the prophets reinterpreted old traditions."[9]

The prophet always felt himself in continuity with the older traditions even as he was radically reinterpreting what he received. Isaiah senses that, as a prophet, he must reinterpret, sometimes even reverse, traditional meanings, because of a new historical situation. The very fact that an oracle needed reinterpretation was a sign that the original situation was a thing of the past. "The history of Jahwism," writes von Rad, "is thus characterized by repeated breaks. God appoints new institutions and fresh starts, which inaugurates new eras of tradition."[10] And elsewhere: "The way in which tradition mounts and grows can be closely followed in the prophetic writings. Exegesis must be less ready than at present to look on this infusion of new blood into the prophetic tradition as 'spurious' or an unhappy distortion of the original. The process is in reality a sign of the living force with which the old message was handed on and adapted to new situations."[11]

## TWO CASES IN THE HISTORY OF CHRISTIANITY

When we turn the Eusebian picture of Christianity on its head, and look at the developments within Christianity from the perspective of where Christianity has gone or is going, we see many of the same characteristics von Rad saw in ancient Israel. The controversies in the history of Christianity are less a testimony to the perseverance of an original faith, as Eusebius would have it, than they are to the place of novelty, change, and innovation. The new has been, on balance, more acceptable to Christians than the old, even though they have claimed otherwise. Let us consider two cases in the history of Christianity.

At the end of the first century, Christianity was a tiny, unknown, unsophisticated religious sect whose future was very uncertain. Christian communities lived very much in a world of their own making on the edge of society, and drew their members from only a small segment of the populace. Most Christians were uneducated, frequently fanatical in their religious practices, and in the words of the Romans, a somewhat depraved, superstitious cult.

Celsus, an informed critic of Christianity, wrote in the mid-second century. "In private homes we see wool-workers, cobblers, handy workers, and the most illiterate and bucolic yokels, who would not dare to say anything at all in front of their elders and more intelligent masters. But whenever they get hold of children in private and some stupid women with them, they let out some astounding statements as, for example, that they must not pay any attention to their father and school-teachers, but must obey them; they say that these talk nonsense and have no understanding, and that in reality they neither know nor are able to do anything good, but are taken up with empty chatter. But they alone, they say, know the right way to live, and if the children would believe them, they would become happy and make their home happy as well. And if just as they are speaking they see one of the school-teachers coming, or some intelligent person, or even the father himself, the more cautious of them flee in all directions; but the more reckless urge the children on to rebel. They whisper to them that in the presence of their father and their schoolmasters they do not feel able to explain anything to the children, since they do not want to have anything to do with the silly and obtuse teachers who are totally corrupted and far gone in wickedness and who inflict punishment on the children. But, if they like, they should leave father and their schoolmasters, and go along with the women and little children who are their play-fellows to the wooldresser's shop, or the cobbler's, or the washerwoman's shop, that they may learn perfection. And by saying this they persuade them."

Most Christians probably fitted this caricature, and even more significantly, liked being considered unlettered. They even made a virtue of their lack of sophistication by quoting the New Testament. In answer to questions about

the reasons behind Christian beliefs, some Christians replied, "Simply believe. Your faith will save you." Or "The
wisdom of this world is foolishness." Proud of their isolation from the surrounding culture, many Christians
thumbed their noses at the autocrats and intellectuals.
Confident they had found a way of life better than their
fellows, they were content to remain in their ghettos. Exploited and abused by the upper classes, these people now
had their own franchise on truth and were not about to
let it be taken over by others.[12]

In this milieu, some other Christians took a hard look
at the church of their day and the received tradition and
concluded that in its present form it could never make its
way in Greco-Roman society. If Christianity did not reinterpret both its tradition and its image, it could make no
sense to the Greco-Roman world, and eventually it would
die.

Justin Martyr, a Christian writing in mid-second century, took the initial step of presenting Christianity not as
an exclusive religious tradition derived largely from Judaism, but as a new philosophical way of life in competition with Stoics, Platonists, Cynics, and the other ruling
"ways" of his day. What would Paul, whose scorn for
philosophy only served to support Justin's critics, have
thought of Christianity as a philosophical sect? The term
"philosophy" appears only seldom in Christian writings up
to this time, and where it appears it is usually regarded
with contempt. Justin, however, believed that the Christian
way of life, as well as the Christian belief about Jesus,
could be tested at the universal bar of reason.[13]

No one before him had really thought seriously of presenting Christianity as a philosophy, but this "innovation," after much opposition, came to be tolerated, accepted, and finally celebrated by Christians of every stripe —from learned theologians to the cobblers, washerwomen, and wool-workers Celsus made fun of. We probably owe the survival of Christianity as a religion within the Roman Empire to this reinterpretation of the earlier Christian beliefs. Now Christianity could present itself as a legitimate way of life whose teaching had the power to rescue men from evil and turn them to lives of goodness and virtue. A "philosophy," wrote Origen in the middle of the third century, "should be approved on the ground that its doctrine . . . had the power to change men from evil." This, Origen was convinced, had happened with the coming of Jesus. The novel idea, that Christianity was a philosophy, at first met with abuse in many circles, but it became the standard way Christian apologists presented their faith to critics. As philosophers, the Christians could claim that they were just as capable of producing men of piety as any of the other religious groups in the empire.[14] Christian apologists altered fundamentally the relation of early Christianity to ancient culture.


THE NICENE CONTROVERSY

The Nicene controversy is another example of how what at first was considered a novelty eventually became accepted as true and orthodox. From the very beginning, the Christian tradition had struggled with the question of

Jesus' relation to God. Jesus was a man born of a woman, nurtured in the home of his parents, taught a trade; he ate, drank, grew weary, experienced pain and suffering, cherished friendships, had enemies, and he died. But he was no ordinary man, as his miracles testified and his Resurrection demonstrated. Very early Christians tried to account for his extraordinary life and accomplishments and his Resurrection, and it was not long before he was called Son of God—then God. Even so, he was not God in the sense in which the Father was God—or was he? Was he creator, was he eternal, should he be addressed in prayer? These and other questions troubled thoughtful Christians for almost three centuries. During these years, most Christians vaguely thought of Jesus as God; yet they did not actually think of him in the same way as they thought of God the Father. They seldom addressed prayers to him, and thought of him somehow as second to God—divine, yes, but not fully God. When men put their minds to the question, it proved unfathomable, for if Jesus was truly God, does that mean that Christians believe in two Gods? Is not God one, simple, undivided? If there are two gods, is not this a return to polytheism and paganism?

When the controversy over the relation of Jesus to God the Father broke out in the early fourth century, most Christians were "subordinationists," i.e. they believed that Christ was God but not in precisely the same way that the Father was God. As we saw in chapter four, the controversy over the Trinity arose when Arius, an unknown priest from Alexandria, entered the picture. He believed in the traditional Christian formulation about Christ, and had been influenced, like most priests and bishops, by Origen, the great Christian thinker who had lived in Alexandria a century earlier. Traditional Christian language and thought asserted that God the Father was absolutely unique and transcendent, alone perfect, alone one, alone sovereign, eternal, wise, and good, alone unchanging. All other beings were second to God, for they owed their existence to him, and unlike him, they came into existence at a particular moment in time. Arius took this traditional understanding of God to mean that Christ, the Word, or Son, of God, had come into being at a particular moment by a creative act of God the Father. Unlike the Father, the Son was "created," and there was a time when he did not exist. He was not eternal. Arius based his views on the traditional Christian view of God's transcendence, and for this reason, his views, especially in modified form, received a wide hearing and gained much support, especially among bishops in the Eastern half of the empire. Arius was a traditionalist.

The problem raised by Arius became particularly acute because Christians were unclear in their own minds how they should express the relation between the Son and the Father. Christian tradition did not give an unambiguous answer. On the one hand, it wished to preserve the traditional belief in God's transcendence, but, on the other hand, it realized that other elements of the tradition suggested that Christ was also fully God. He was thought, for example, to have taken part in the creation of the world. The Gospel of John quotes Jesus as saying, "I and the Father are one." For centuries, Christians had been baptizing "in the name of the Father and of the Son and of the Holy Spirit." No distinction seems to be made between the Father, on the one hand, and the Son and the Spirit, on the other. Yet Jesus was clearly a man, as the Gospels testified; he was born, he grew, he grew weary, he hungered, he did not know all things, he suffered, and he died. How, then, can he be fully God if he is described as doing and participating so fully in the world of change? God, by definition, does not change.

The council of Nicaea decided that the Son was to be considered fully God in the same way that God the Father was God. "We believe in one Lord Jesus Christ, the Son of God, begotten of the Father, the only begotten, that is from the being of the Father, God from God, Light from Light, true God from true God, begotten not made, of one substance (*homoousios*) with the Father. . . ." The term *homoousios* used in the creed, and the idea behind it, were revolutionary in the history of Christian thought. John did not mean what the fourth-century fathers meant by *homoousios* when he attributed to Jesus the words "I and the Father are one." John was not even thinking of the problem raised by the dispute in the early fourth century. And some earlier Christian writers had actually rejected the term as unsuitable to describe the relation between the Son and the Father.

In the second and third centuries, Christian thinkers, especially the apologists, had used the language of Platonism to express the relation between the Son and the Father. In Platonic thought it was possible to speak of a hierarchy of being within the Godhead. That is, things could be either more or less divine. Angels and heavenly beings, for example, were thought to be divine, but they were not thought to be divine in the sense in which God the Father was divine. There were different levels of divinity stretching up to the source of all divinity, God himself. Behind these ideas lay the conviction that the truly divine characteristic was to be the source, the origin, the beginning of all things. God was, therefore, divine in that all things came from him and had their ultimate source in him. But there could be only *one* source, for if there were two sources, what was the source and origin of the two? In this scheme, Christ, the Son of God, the Logos (i.e. the Word of God), was thought to be the highest and most perfect of all divine beings, but not God in the full sense of being the source and origin of all things.

The council of Nicaea dealt with this problem by determining that the Son was not to be considered the highest and best of divine beings, i.e. at the peak of the hierarchy of being, but that he was to be considered of the same substance, of the being, of God the source and origin of all things. The Son was not part of those things "made" by God, but himself creator and maker. They rejected the idea of a hierarchy of being and any suggestion that the Son was a third element between the transcendent God and the created world.

It has been fashionable to view the Nicene council as proof of the Hellenization of the gospel. Did not the fathers at Nicaea introduce a non-biblical term, *homoousios,* and with it certain Greek ideas to explain and interpret the Christian faith? Is not Nicaea an example of how the simple faith of the Bible became encrusted within the philosophical and intellectual categories of Greek metaphysics?

Perhaps, but I think it more likely that the reverse is true. Nicaea is an attempt on the part of Christian thinkers to think through the implications of their faith in light of the difficulties that had arisen *because* the Christian tradition had used Greek categories for several centuries. This is not to say that Nicaea is a return to an earlier biblical view of God and the relation of the Son to the Father. The biblical writers simply did not think about these problems, and would have been baffled by the questions of the fourth century. Nicaea is a new stage in the history of Christian thinking. It represents a new way of looking at the relation of the Son to the Father in light of the biblical tradition *and* the ideas Christians had learned from the Greek philosophical tradition. The council of Nicaea and the debates that followed it introduced something *new* into the Christian tradition. Athanasius and his supporters, in spite of their protestations to the contrary, are the innovators in the fourth century.[15]

Nicaea also led to other innovations. Once the new understanding of the Son came to be accepted, men began to wonder about the Holy Spirit. We saw in chapter four how Basil defended his views on the Holy Spirit against the charge that they were innovations. In his defense he engaged in endless controversy and wrote a book on the Holy Spirit, the only systematic treatise on the subject from the early church. If the Son was *homoousios* with the Father, it would seem that the Spirit, too, was *homoousios*.

Basil tried to show how this new idea squared with earlier tradition and with the Bible, but his opponents were correct—the earliest Christian writings simply do not think of the Spirit in the way Basil proposed. Nevertheless, Basil's innovation came to be accepted by most Christians, and by the early fifth century the belief in the divinity of the Holy Spirit was considered orthodox and apostolic Christian teaching. The innovations of one generation became in time identical with the ancient and original Christian faith.

### DIVERSITY AND COMMON IDENTITY

A missionary to the Germans in the seventh century, a hermit in the Egyptian desert, a bishop in a Byzantine court, a Spanish peasant, a Renaissance prince, an African tribesman, a twentieth-century electrical engineer, a suburban housewife in southern California—all these people have claimed the name Christian, but their style of Christian life and what they would identify as Christian would have little in common. They may all agree: "God is one, Jesus is his instrument among men, we should be faithful to Jesus." But if we try to reduce the variety of Christian experience to its common denominator, we tend to speak trivialities. More importantly, we miss the distinctiveness of the various witnesses from the Christian past. Men can be, and often have been, faithful Christians with radically different, even contradictory, ways of life and beliefs. Yet they feel a bond with each other and a common identity. No one idea can embrace all, and what may work for one group, one generation, or even for whole centuries, will surely give way at a later time to something new. Indeed, the one sure thing that we learn from Christian history is that Christianity is always changing, in spite of the protestations of Christians to the reverse. They have managed to keep their identity amidst the most radical changes of practice, belief, thought, and institutions.

There is no original Christian faith, no native language, no definitive statement of the meaning of Christ for all times. The dialectic of past and present, tradition and innovation, permanence and change, runs through the whole history of Christianity. What is regarded as novel to one generation becomes authoritative tradition to another. Christians have, in their construction of the past, prized antiquity, stability, and permanence, but the historical record shows us quite another picture. Christians have said one thing while going ahead and doing something else. The apostles spoke several languages, and Christians ever since have done the same. No matter how deeply we probe, how early we extend our search, we will never find an original faith. We can't go home again, not only because the home we once knew has changed beyond recognition. No, there never was a home. From the beginning, Christians have been wanderers and pilgrims whose dream lies not in the past, but before them and all men—in the future.

## CHAPTER VIII

## What Has Been
## Is Not What Will Be

To the accompaniment of a rock beat, the pop singers Zager and Evans, in the best-selling record "2525," portray man's future over the next eight thousand years. In the year 5555 "your arms are hanging limp at your side, your legs got nothing to do, some machine doing that for you." In the year 6565 "you ain't gonna need no husband, won't need no wife, you'll pick your son and daughter from the bottom of a long glass tube." In the year 8510 "God is going to shake his mighty head, he'll either say 'I'm pleased where man has been' or tear it down and start again."

Men do not as a rule contemplate such distant futures, 3000 or 6000 years hence. We are more inclined to speculate about population growth over the next generation, the size of the Gross National Product in 1980, the state of medical science in the year 2000, or even the level of pollution in the Hudson River by 1990. As predictable and prosaic as these projections may be, they reflect man's awareness that time moves ceaselessly on, and that human life is not fulfilled in the past or present. Even though man may have no gift of prophecy or augury, he senses that the meaning of life lies ahead of him. His hopes and dreams, his plans and projects, have meaning only insofar as there is a future.

In the preceding chapters we have seen how the Eusebian model of Christianity made the time of origins—the beginning, the apostolic age—the decisive moment in the history of Christianity. The metaphor of virginity, suggested as early as the second century by a Christian author, symbolized this view. Perfection, completeness, wholeness lay in the past at the beginning, and the historical development of Christianity took the form of a movement away from the original perfection or an attempt to return to it. Eusebianism has no place for genuine change or newness, which is to say it has no place for the future. Nothing really new happens in the history of Christianity, because everything is given at the beginning. In the words of Ecclesiastes: "What has been is what will be, and what has been done is what will be done."

The Eusebian construction of the past, like many theological and historical ideas, has been handed on from generation to generation as a self-evident truth. But like most theological ideas, it has a history. The Christian idea of the Incarnation, for example, arose at a particular stage in Christian thought to account for the extraordinary life of Jesus and his Resurrection. How could an ordinary man born of a woman teach as he did, do such marvels, and overcome the power of death? To answer these questions, Christians said that Jesus was God's pre-existent Son, who had come to live among men as a man. In the birth of Jesus, God's Son had taken on human flesh, i.e. become incarnate. Incarnation is a theological conception used to interpret the meaning of Jesus' life, but in normal Christian usage the term is used carelessly to refer to the historical event of his birth, as one refers to the historical event of his baptism, his trial, or his death. The theological idea became in the course of time identical with the historical event of the birth of Jesus of Nazareth from Mary.

Similarly, the Eusebian construction of the past has, over the course of centuries, become identical with the historical events surrounding the beginning of Christianity. What is historically evident is that there was a first generation of Christians, but in Christian language and thought these first years are identified with an idealized conception of an apostolic age. We have seen that this way of constructing Christian origins arose at a particular time under specific circumstances, gradually took hold in the Christian consciousness, and eventually wove itself into the fabric of Christian experience and thought.

Arising as it did in the spiritual climate of late antiquity, the Eusebian model of Christianity took on some of the contours of ancient ideas of truth. Truth was thought to be older than error, and men who lived in earlier times, especially at the very beginning, were thought to live closer to the gods. In the Christian view, divine revelation was thought to have ceased with the death of the last apostle. Implicitly, and often explicitly, the past became the judge of the present and future. But as time went on, the apostles could not answer every question, meet every crisis, or solve every dilemma faced by Christians. Though primary authority was always thought to rest first and foremost with the apostles, their authority was extended to certain later writers, to bishops gathering in council, and to certain institutions such as the episcopacy or the papacy. Neither council nor bishop nor pope ever dared to claim that his authority was higher than that of the apostles, yet councils, bishops, and popes often had to take upon themselves the responsibility of defining what the apostles meant in cases in which they had spoken not at all or only in whispers.

Later generations, looking back on the writings of the fathers, conciliar decrees, and papal letters, gave to these documents an authority almost paralleling that of the apostles. "They themselves were not the speakers, but the Spirit of God," said one early Christian author. The cumulative effect of extending apostolic authority into later Christian history was to accentuate the authoritative role of the past in Christian thinking. Scripture and tradition became the accepted tests of Christian truth.

## TRANSCENDING THE PRESENT

The Christian construction of history serves as a constant reminder that Christianity did not begin just yesterday. This is, of course, obvious to every Christian. Yet its significance should not be overlooked. The Christian community, through its construction of the past, brings to consciousness the conviction that what it believes, teaches, and practices does not spring up anew with each generation. There is continuity from one age to the next, and the present is not the sum of all that is. The sense of a common past, a past shared by countless different kinds of people, gives to the Christian community a sense of who it is, a sense of its identity. "When amnesia comes upon a generation of Christians," wrote Albert Outler, "when they are unmindful of who they were, or what they have as their rightful legacy from the total Christian past, it is all too easy to concentrate on who they are now and to magnify the distance between themselves and other Christians. . . . Both the unity and vitality of Christianity depend upon a common memory, a common hope—and a common faith rooted in that memory."[1]

In an age in which men worship the goddess Now and serve her in a cult of Relevance, it is well to remind ourselves that the value of the historical memory of a religious tradition is that it allows men to meet their age in a perspective that transcends their times. A people without a historical memory is like a country with no roads to guide the traveler.

### THE GREAT FALLACY

Christians have, however, claimed more. By constructing an authoritative past, they have said not simply that the past provides them with a road map of the Christian nation, but that it also provides a list of which roads one should take and which ones one should avoid. In the Eusebian view, the past assumes the role of an *imperative* for present and future. Whatever was a genuine mark of Christianity in the past *should* also mark the church of the present. What *should be* is derived from what *was*.[2]

The great fallacy of Eusebianism is that it inverts the order of historical experience.

"Historical phenomena," wrote Rudolf Bultmann in his Gifford lectures on history and eschatology, "are not what they are in pure isolation, but only in relation to the future for which they have importance. We say: To each historical phenomenon belongs its future, a future in which alone it will appear as that which it really is—to speak precisely we must say: the future in which it evermore appears as that which it is."[3]

We cannot fully understand a historical phenomenon by uncovering its origin; we must also look at what became of it, what twists and turns it took in the course of its history, and what came from it. What it *is* can never be derived from what it has been; for what something *is* continually changes as the present and future unfolds before it. How partial and fragmentary the biography of a man if it is written at, let us say, age twenty. What someone or something will be can never be divorced from what it *was,* but the future constantly offers new promise and possibilities that are frequently inexplicable on the basis of what was in the past or is in the present.

The strength of the Eusebian view is that it recognizes the role of the past in defining what it means to be Christian. It gives a clear answer to the question, What is Christianity? Eusebius said that the marks of true Christianity can be found written in the past. The great debates in the history of Christianity have been, in large measure, debates about the meaning of the past, i.e. the meaning of the Bible and tradition. But these debates have also been debates about the *present* and the *future*. What are we to say or think in this new situation? How are we to act in light of this new set of circumstances? Whether the question was the doctrine of the Trinity in the early church, the investiture of bishops and abbots by princes and emperors in the Middle Ages, the meaning of the "gospel" in the Reformation, or the role of the church in society in our day, the issues arose out of the *present*. The answers, too, arose out of the present, as a new generation of Christians confronted their own age. They met the challenge of their times not as disembodied spirits, but as participants in the life of their own age *and* as living bearers of a tradition extending back thousands of years. The answers they gave and the solutions they offered arose out of their memory of Jesus as this memory was handed on by the apostles and fathers, but the answers they gave were their own.

The Eusebian construction of the history of Christianity robs the present and future of meaning, for it will not allow historical experience to contribute anything to that which was given at the beginning. For this reason, Eusebianism cannot account for change and diversity—the newness brought by each generation of Christians as it confronts its own age. As a first step in constructing a new historical picture of Christianity, I would suggest that we turn the whole history of Christianity on its end. Instead of viewing the Christian history as a movement *away from* something—an original perfection—why not view it as a movement *toward* something? Perfection lies, if anywhere, not at the beginning, but at the end. The stumbling efforts of Christians to embody their vision of God in ideas and concepts, in institutions, in morals and actions, and in customs and liturgy, are the striving, the reaching forward, indeed the longing, of men for something that is not yet realized and has never been realized in human history. The Christian dreams of things that never were. What has been is not what will be; and what will be never was—to turn the words of Ecclesiastes topsy-turvy.

## THE CHRISTIAN VISION

The Christian vision of man, of the world, of society, has always transcended every historical expression, because it arises out of a vision of God. The Christian vision springs from Jesus' proclamation of the Kingdom of God, and the Christian hope in this Kingdom rests on the Resurrection of Jesus from the dead. Jesus' Resurrection did not usher in the Kingdom of God on earth, but it began something new in human experience and gave men reason to believe that their hope in the Kingdom was not misplaced. Because Jesus' Resurrection did not establish the Kingdom, there is no warrant for Christians to look back and say, "Lo, here" or "Lo, there." All historical forms, ideas, or expressions are at best "penultimate." "The Kingdom reveals itself again and again as still unrealized future that confronts every present and that will confront a, hopefully, better future situation. This futurity of the Kingdom opens ever new possibilities for action while still denying any human institution the glory of perfection that might

warrant its making an absolute claim on the obedience
of individuals."[4]

What might it mean to view the history of Christianity as a movement *toward* something rather than a movement *away* from something? 1. Christianity cannot be
defined by its origins alone. 2. We cannot escape the consequences of our history by the construction of an idealized concept of "true" Christianity given in the past. 3. The
past is not the judge of the present or the future.

OUR POST-CONSTANTINIAN AGE

1. When Christianity began as a sect within Judaism,
no one could have conceived that this tiny band of Jews
would become the religion of Western civilization. But
the sect that sprang up in Palestine gave way within two
hundred years to a universal religion deeply impregnated
with the cultural and philosophical concepts of the Greco-
Roman world. At a later date this same religion won over
most of the citizens of the Roman Empire to its faith, and
by the year four hundred it had become the official religion of the Roman Empire. The history of Christianity
and the history of Western civilization are from that period until the eighteenth century one story. Quite simply,
this means that whatever Christianity was at its beginning,
in the course of time it became the church of popes and
cardinals, of prime ministers and kings, of priests blessing
cannons in battle, of Crusades and wars of religion, the
paintings of Giotto, the sculpture and architecture of Ber-
nini, and the music of Bach. The tiny house churches of

the first years of Christianity did become the institutions we today know as the Episcopal, Methodist, Roman Catholic, and Orthodox Christian churches.

It is part of the rhetoric of the mid-twentieth century that we live in a post-Constantinian age. Christianity, we are told, is no longer the official religion of our civilization, and even more important, it is no longer the dominant spiritual force shaping the life of society and the ideals of our culture. The demise of the Constantinian epoch has been as naïvely celebrated by modern religious thinkers as its commencement was heralded by Eusebius in the fourth century. Whatever the merits of designating our age as post-Constantinian—and there are merits—what many people seem to forget is that it is post-*Constantinian,* i.e. after *Constantine.* Presumably it makes some difference for Christianity that Constantine reigned for 1500 years. Christianity is no longer and can never become again the tiny charismatic religious movement we identify with the first Christian communities. This is not to say that it cannot be charismatic, but charisma has to take quite a different form when Billy Graham serves as court preacher to the President of the United States and Terence Cardinal Cooke is the celebrated vicar of the Armed Forces. Things can never be quite the same once a scarlet-robed cardinal crowns a king, even if the cardinal may, at a later time, go into hiding because the king persecutes him.

Christianity is different, because it passed through the Constantinian age. Whether one likes what resulted from the Constantinian epoch or not, the establishment of

Christianity as the religion of the Roman Empire is a testimony to the conviction of ancient Christians that God is the God of all men and that his rule should extend to social, political, and cultural life. Partial and frail though their efforts may have been, they were the attempts of men to understand and embody in their lives and institutions their vision of a God who transcended the limits of their minds and experiences. As a consequence of their dream of the unity of mankind in the worship of the one God, we live in a civilization that has been molded by Christian ideals and in churches shaped by the values of Western civilization. The 1500 years stand before us as a part of the historical record, and therefore as part of the definition of what it *is* to be Christian in the twentieth century.

CHRISTIAN ANTI-SEMITISM

2. The belief in an idealized past has made it too easy for Christians to sidestep the consequences of their own historical development. If "true" Christianity is identified with an ideal given in the past, it is apparent that Christians must exclude those segments of the past that do not correspond to this idea, i.e. those that are antithetical to true Christianity and therefore aberrations. We have seen how the classical historical works treated heresy and the way Reformation historians treated their opponents. Let us take a more contemporary example.

Christians have been charged with being anti-Semitic. As we observed in the first chapter, recent studies confirm this impression. To varying degrees, Christians of every stripe have been shown to be anti-Semitic in their attitudes and patterns of behavior.[5] Furthermore, Christian anti-Semitism did not arise by the importation of ideas foreign to Christianity through some historical accident. Christian anti-Semitism grew out of the Christian Bible, i.e. the New Testament, as it was understood and interpreted by Christians over centuries. The roots of Christian anti-Semitism need be traced no further than Christianity itself; Christians have been anti-Semitic because they have been Christians. They thought of themselves as the people of God, the true Israel, who had been faithful to the inheritance of ancient Israel. Judaism, in the Christian view, had no reason to exist once Christianity came on the scene. We must learn, I think, to live with the unpleasant fact that anti-Semitism is part of what it has meant historically to be a Christian, and is still part of what it means to be Christian.

Christians react to this predicament in various ways.[6] Some pretend that the church fathers did not mean what they said about the Jews. Others simply ignore what has been said, or try to forget. Others say that some Christians may indeed be anti-Semitic, that in fact many Christians may have been anti-Semitic, but that these Christians represent an aberration from authentic Christianity, not true Christian attitudes. Insofar as they are anti-Semitic, they are not good Christians; so goes the argument. The last ploy is the most frequent and most familiar. It has been used over and over by Christians to escape the consequences of the historical development of the Christian religion. Invariably, Christians turn to the New Testament and ask, Is the New Testament anti-Semitic?—assuming that if it is not, then Christianity is not anti-Semitic. (Whether or not the New Testament is anti-Semitic is not the point at issue here.) Usually the answer is "No," and an "ideal" Christianity—not anti-Semitic—is taken as the true form of Christian faith. Any deviation from the ideal can then be dismissed because it is not authentically Christian.

What the first Christians thought about Jews is an interesting, and I think important, issue, but what happened to their thoughts in the later history of Christianity is infinitely more significant for understanding and interpreting the Christian movement. If we take seriously the historical character of Christianity, we will have to recognize that the only Christianity there is, is the Christianity of our historical experience. Even if we could show that Christians were not anti-Semitic at the beginning, it would not alter the fact that Christians today are shaped by a religious tradition that tolerates and encourages anti-Semitic attitudes. By identifying true Christianity with an ideal in the past, Eusebius gave to Christians an easy way out of serious historical criticism.

### THE PAST IS NEVER THE WHOLE STORY

3. The past is not the judge of the future. This is simply another way of saying that the meaning of the past constantly changes as new historical experience unfolds before us. We view earlier history in light of what comes

later, not the later in light of what was earlier. What becomes of a historical phenomenon will provide the basis on which we interpret its significance. We have all seen rigged statistics that show only part of the story, or we have looked at graphs that are cut off at precisely the right point to create the impression that the progress is steadily upward. Likewise, to cut off the development of a historical phenomenon before it has run its course, or to lift up one period early in the history as "normative," not only alters our perspective, it actually falsifies that which we see.

At one time, Mithraism was the chief rival of Christianity in the Roman Empire, but, fifteen hundred years later, Mithraism is an interesting historical curiosity for specialists in the study of ancient religion, whereas Christianity is a living faith embracing millions of men. This does not mean that Christianity is better than Mithraism; but it does mean that the historical significance of each religion is quite different from what it would have been if Mithraism had survived and Christianity had not.

We can never plan the future in terms of the past. The past tells us where we have been, what we have done, and how we have come to be what we are. But it can never tell us what we will be. It is, in short, *indicative*. Who would have thought in the late nineteenth century, when Protestant Christianity was so closely identified with Americanism, that in mid-twentieth century the same churches would become the centers of protest against American chauvinism? We can never define what it is that is uniquely Christian for all times, because what *Christi-*

*anity* is continues to change. The past may suggest what we might be, but it can never become an *imperative* for future action. (Anyone who deals in mutual funds knows that how a fund has performed in the past is simply that: how it has performed in the past. It does suggest how it may perform in the future, but there is no assurance that it will perform as it has.) The past is never the whole story. It is, in the language of our technological society, one of the inputs fed into the computer; but there are other inputs, and what comes out is not the same as the experience we fed into it.[7]

The works of the present do not need to be justified by an appeal to an authoritative past. I am reminded of a story once told me by Rabbi Irwin Blank of Tenafly, New Jersey. On a certain occasion, Rabbi Eliezer used all possible arguments to substantiate his opinion, but the rabbis did not accept it. He said, "If I am right, may this carob tree move a hundred yards from its place." It did so. . . . They said, "From a tree no proof can be brought." Then he said, "May the canal prove it." The water of the canal flowed backward. They said, "Water cannot prove anything." Then he said, "May the walls of this House of Study prove it." Then the walls of the house bent inward, as if they were about to fall. Rabbi Joshua rebuked the walls, and said to them, "If the learned dispute about the Halakah, what has that to do with you?" So, to honor Rabbi Joshua, the walls did not fall down, but to honor Rabbi Eliezer, they did not become quite straight again. Then Rabbi Eliezer said, "If I am right, let the heavens prove it." Then Rabbi Joshua got up and said, "It is not in heaven." (Deuteronomy XXX, 12) What did he mean by this? Rabbi Jeremiah said, "The law was given us from Sinai. We pay no attention to a heavenly voice. For already from Sinai the Law said, 'By a majority you are to decide.'" Rabbi Nathan met Elijah and asked him what God did in that hour. Elijah replied, "He laughed and said, 'My children have conquered me.'"[8]

When his children conquer him, God does not always laugh. When Jesus appeared in the little Spanish town in the sixteenth century in Dostoevsky's *The Brothers Karamazov,* the Grand Inquisitor told him: "At last we have completed the work begun in your name. For fifteen centuries we have been wrestling with your freedom, but now it is ended and over for good. . . . You promised them the bread of Heaven . . . but can it compare with earthly bread in the eyes of the weak, ever sinful and ignoble race of man? . . . We have corrected your work and have founded it upon miracle, mystery and authority." The tale of the Grand Inquisitor reminds us that neither rosy optimism about the future nor naïve celebration of change for the sake of change has place in the Christian experience. The history of Christianity is not an unrestricted march of progress toward some future good. The good has been—and is—more elusive than that. Change in itself is by no means a supreme virtue. Change does not always bring change for the better; there can be change for the worse. The problem with the Grand Inquisitor, in our view, is not that he was unfaithful to the past, but that he was unfaithful to the future.

# EPILOGUE

Like a good story, the value of the past lies in the telling, not in the moral drawn from the tale. The past gives no authority and yields no imperative save that it is there. It happened and it is remembered. We learn from the past, but what we learn is always tempered by who we are, when we live, and what we anticipate. The moral, to continue the analogy of the story, comes from the storyteller. The meanings we assign to the past arise out of the crucible of the present and our hopes for the future. The moral keeps changing because we keep changing. Even the professional historian, trained to approach his task with scientific precision and accuracy, realizes that the historical memory of the same events changes as it is filtered through the experience of a new generation of historians. How differently the Reformation looks, now that Protestants and Catholics view it as brothers. It is not so much that the sources for Reformation history have changed—though this is partly true—but that we have changed.

The things for which Christians give themselves in 1970 are not the same things for which they gave themselves in 1870, 1070, or 70, and they should not be the same for which they give themselves in 2070. Christians march to different drums today; but since the beginning of Christianity, the drumbeats have been changing. The dreams Christians have in the latter half of the twentieth century—dreams of peace, of social justice, of freedom, of the unity of all Christians, of personal and psychological wholeness, of community among all men—arise out of the experience of twenty centuries, but they are not really to be found in the past.

If we deny to the events of the past the right to plan our future, we do not simply relegate the experience of former generations to the ash heap of antiquity. Nor do we flatten out every historical moment as though the past were one monotonous, gray plain. The Christian memory is unique, singular, and particular. There are still mountains and valleys and plateaus. What we remember, and how we remember it, will change, but the Christian memory will always trace its origins to the tiny band of Jews who walked with Jesus, lived through his death, witnessed his Resurrection, and proclaimed his glory to all the world.

But the Christian hope is set on things that never were. Christians have no more knowledge of what lies ahead for mankind or for themselves than anyone else. They are privy to no private revelations of what will be someday. Yet, like all men, they live and act on the basis of a future they do not know. Their dreams of what will be, ricochet back to them to create things they have never known before. Unlike a boomerang that is thrown into the air to return the same as it was thrown, man's dreams and fantasies fly back to him not only to create realities from what were once only dreams, but to surprise him with undreamt-of realities. We may identify our ideals with particular pasts, but as much as the past may give specificity and concreteness to our dreams, what men dream, what they hope for, does not spring from the past. The artist, trained in the methods of his predecessors, goes on to create out of his own imagination works of beauty unlike any that men created before him.

The Christian realizes that his history goes back to the time of the apostles, but he also knows that the Christian hope did not come to fulfillment in the age of the apostles; nor did it reach perfection at the time of Constantine, nor in the Holy Roman Empire of the Middle Ages, nor in the sixteenth-century Reformation, nor in the social gospel of the late nineteenth century or the revivals on the American frontier, nor in the movements of renewal in our own day. The history of Christianity is the history of imperfection and fragmentation, but it is also a history of hoping and striving for an end men cannot see but that draws them on. The future constantly opens up new possibilities that make the past look pale by comparison.

Gregory of Nyssa, a Christian theologian of the fourth century, once compared God to a spring bubbling out of the earth. "As you came near the spring you would marvel, seeing that the water was endless, as it constantly gushed up and poured forth. Yet you could never say that you had seen all the water. How could you see what was still hidden in the bosom of the earth? Hence no matter how long you might stay at the spring you would always be beginning to see the water. For the water never stops flowing, and it is always beginning to bubble up again. It is the same with one who fixes his gaze on the infinite beauty of God. It is constantly being discovered anew, and it is always seen as something new and strange in comparison with what the mind has already understood. And as God continues to reveal himself, man continues to wonder; and he never exhausts his desire to see more, since what he is waiting for is always more magnificent, more divine, than all that he has already seen."[1]

God is always being discovered anew. Men have seen his works in the past, but his fullness always lies ahead of us. God's Kingdom, as present as it was in the life of Jesus, was still future to Jesus. It was future to the apostles, to the fathers and schoolmen, to the reformers and popes; it was future to our fathers, and it is future to us. Our age is not subject to the works of the past; it is subject only to the dreams of the future. One day our generation, like that of the apostles, of Augustine and Justinian, of Thomas and Calvin, of John Wesley and Thomas Campbell, will be *past* to a future we do not know. If the Christian hope is a vision of God, the imperfections of the present are not deviations from an original Christian faith but the unfinished and unformed experiences of men and women whose lives point to a God who is infinitely more beautiful, infinitely more gracious, and infinitely more true than anything any man has ever known. "Remember not the former things, nor consider the things of old. Behold, I am doing a new thing; now it springs forth, do you not perceive it?" (Isaiah 43:18–19)

# NOTES

## Chapter I

1. Richard Hofstadter, *The Progressive Historians* (New York, 1968), p. 3.
2. See Henry Steele Commager, "The Search for a Usable Past," *American Heritage* 16, 2 (February 1965), pp. 6 ff.
3. Woodrow Wilson and Albert Beveridge, cited in Ernest L. Tuveson, *Redeemer Nation: the Idea of America's Millenial Role* (Chicago, 1968), pp. 211, vii.
4. Report published in the New York *Times,* June 6, 1969, p. 23.
5. See the chapter "From Coercion to Persuasion" in Sidney E. Mead's *The Lively Experiment* (New York, 1963), pp. 16–37.
6. Mircea Eliade, *Cosmos and History* (New York, 1959), pp. 44–46.
7. Alfred Schutz, "Don Quixote and the Problem of Reality," *Collected Papers II* (The Hague, 1964), pp. 135–58. See also the writings of Maurice Halbwachs, *Les Cadres Sociaux de la Mémoire* (Paris, 1925); *La Mémoire Collective* (Paris, 1950); also his interesting work on the shifting topography of the Holy Land as the "collective memory, essentially a reconstruction of the past, adapted the image of the ancient facts to the beliefs and spiritual needs of the present. . . ." *La Topographie Légendaire des Évangiles en Terre Sainte. Étude de Mémoire Collective* (Paris, 1941), p. 9; also Peter Berger and Thomas Luckmann, *The Social Construction of Reality* (New York,

1966; Peter Berger, *The Sacred Canopy* (New York, 1969; published in London as *The Social Reality of Religion.*

8. Charles Y. Glock and Rodney Stark, *Christian Beliefs and Anti-Semitism.* Vol. I of a series of the Survey Research Center under a grant from the Anti-Defamation League of B'Nai B'rith (New York, 1966), chapter 4, pp. 60 ff.; on the historical development of these attitudes, see Robert L. Wilken, "Insignissima Religio, Certe Licita? Christianity and Judaism in the Fourth and Fifth Centuries," in Jerald C. Brauer (ed.), *The Impact of the Church on Its Culture* (Chicago, 1968), pp. 36–66.

9. Hans Küng, *The Church* (New York and London 1967), p. 4.

10. See Peter Berger, *The Sacred Canopy*, p. 33.

## CHAPTER II

1. On Luke, see Hans Conzelmann, *The Theology of St. Luke* (London, 1960).

   On Acts, see the commentary by Ernst Haenchen, *Die Apostelgeschichte* (Goettingen, 1957; ET Oxford 1971); Henry J. Cadbury, *The Making of Luke-Acts* (New York and London 1927); Frederick J. Foakes-Jackson and Kirsopp Lake, *The Beginnings of Christianity* (London, 1920–23), five vols.

2. Ernst Haenchen, "Apostelgeschichte," in *Religion in Geschichte und Gegenwart* (Tuebingen, 1957), I, 502.

3. Jean Daniélou and Henri Marrou, *The First Six Hundred Years* (New York and London 1964), p. 3.

4. Ernst Haenchen, *Die Apostelgeschichte*, p. 132.

5. For a collection of these writings, see Edgar Hennecke, *New Testament Apocrypha*, edited by Wilhelm Schneemelcher, translated by R. McL. Wilson (Philadelphia, 1964 and London 1965), Vol. II.

6. For a fuller discussion of these ideas, see R. P. C. Hanson, *Tradition in the Early Church* (Philadelphia and London 1962), H. E. W. Turner, *The Pattern of Christian Truth* (London, 1954), and the bibliography cited in

Robert L. Wilken, "Tertullian and the Early Christian View of Tradition," *Concordia Theological Monthly* 38 (1967), p. 221.

7. "Irenaeus of Lyon Against Heresies" 1.2.3. (ed. Harvey), trans. S. L. Greenslade, *Early Latin Theology* ("Library of Christian Classics" Vol. V; Philadelphia and London 1956), pp. 65–66.

8. Hegesippus is known to us chiefly through fragments preserved in Eusebius' *Ecclesiastical History*, 4.8. 22; 2.23; 3.19. 32. For details of what is known of his life, see William Milligan, "Hegesippus," in *Dictionary of Christian Biography* (London, 1880), II, pp. 875–78.

9. Tertullian, *Prescription Against Heretics* 16 (trans. S. L. Greenslade, *Early Latin Theology*, p. 42).

10. Irenaeus, *Against Heresies* 3.3, *op. cit.*, p. 68.

11. Hegesippus, cited by Eusebius, *Ecclesiastical History*, 4.22.2–3; 22.4–6 (trans. H. J. Lawlor and J. E. L. Oulton [London, 1954], I, pp. 127–28).

12. Tertullian, "Prescription" 9–11; 20–22; 27; 32 et pass.

13. *Ibid.* 29–31.

14. *Ibid.* 30.

15. *Ibid.* 35.

16. See the materials collected in Joseph Vogt, *Ciceros Glaube an Rom* ("Wuerzburger Studien zur Altertumswissenschaft," 6 Heft; Stuttgart, 1935); also Charles Norris Cochrane, *Christianity and Classical Culture* (New York, 1957), ch. 3.

17. Lucretius, *De rerum natura* 5.170 ff.

18. Cicero, *Laws* 2.10(27).

19. Plato, *Philebus* 16c.

In the preface to his *History of Rome*, Livy writes: "Either I am blinded by love for my task, or there never was a state greater, purer and richer in good examples; no community into which avarice and luxury penetrated so late; none where poverty and thrift were for so long held in such high esteem. The fewer our resources, the less there was of cupidity. It is but recently that an accumulation of wealth has stimulated avarice; the superabundance of material goods an itch on the part of men to indulge a passion which is ruinous to everything including themselves." (trans., Charles N. Cochrane, *Christianity and Classical Culture* [New York, 1957], p. 96)

## Chapter III

1. Eusebius, *Ecclesiastical History* (E. H.) 10.1.8 (trans. G. A. Williamson, Middlesex, Penguin Books, 1965, p. 381). On Eusebius' life and works, see the essay by Hans F. von Campenhausen, *The Fathers of the Greek Church* (New York, 1959), pp. 57–66.
   On Eusebius' place in the history of church historical writing, see Ferdinand Christian Baur, *The Epochs of Church Historiography* ("A Library of Protestant Thought," ed. Peter C. Hodgson, New York, 1968), pp. 53–66; more recently, Peter Meinhold, *Geschichte der kirchlichen Historiographie* (Munich, 1967), pp. 95 ff.
2. E. H. 1.1.4 (Williamson), p. 32.
3. Eusebius, citing Porphyry, in *Praeparatio Evangelica*, preface; E. H. 1.4.1. In his letter to his wife, Marcella, Porphyry wrote, "The greatest fruit of piety is to worship God according to the ways of the fathers." (*Ad Marcellam* 18).
4. E. H. 1.4.4–5, 10 (Williamson, pp. 45–47). On Eusebius' *Ecclesiastical History* as an apology for Christianity, see the essay by Jaroslav Pelikan, "Eusebius: Finality and Universality in History," in his *The Finality of Jesus Christ in an Age of Universal History* (Richmond, 1965), pp. 48–57.
5. E. H. 1.1.7–8 (Williamson), p. 33.
6. E. H. 1.1.2 (Williamson), pp. 31–32.
7. E. H. 5.16.10, 28.2; 7.30.4 (trans. H. J. Lawlor and J. E. L. Oulton [London, 1954], I, pp. 172, 160).
8. E. H. 4.8.11; 2.13.5: 6.36.3 et passim.

9. Rufinus, *Comm. in Symb. apost.* 2 (*Patrologia Latina* 21, col. 337); Pseudo-Augustine, "De Symbolo," serm. 240 (*Patrologia Latina* 39, col. 2189). Cited in J. N. D. Kelly, *Early Christian Creeds* (New York, 1960), pp. 1–3.

10. Rufinus, Preface to Origen, *De Principiis*, 2 (G. W. Butterworth, ed. *On First Principles*, New York, 1966), p. lxiii.

11. E. H. 4.29.6; 5.15; 3.38.5; 4.22.1–3.

12. E. H. 3.32.7–8 (Williamson), p. 143.

13. Ferdinand Christian Baur, *Epochs*, p. 60.

14. Erik H. Erikson, *Gandhi's Truth* (New York, 1969), p. 55.

15. E. H. 10.9.7–9 (Williamson), pp. 413–14.

## Chapter IV

1. Ammianus Marcellinus, 21.16.18.

2. Text from minutes of the council in Eduard Schwartz, ed., *Acta Conciliorum Oecumenicorum* (Berlin, 1914 ff.), II, 1, 1, p. 91, ll. 15 ff. For this and other passages discussed in this section, see Robert L. Wilken, "Scripture and Dogma in the Ancient Church," *Lutheran World* 14 (1967), pp. 168 ff.

3. *Acta Conciliorum Oecumenicorum*, II, 1,2, pp. 126–27.

4. *Commonitorium* 2.3; ". . . quod ubique, quod semper, quod ab omnibus creditum est."

5. Cyril of Alexandria, *Paschal Homily* 11.5 (*Patrologia Graeca*, 77, col. 633a); see the material collected in Robert L. Wilken, *Judaism and the Early Christian Mind* (New Haven, 1971), ch. 8.

6. Text in T. Herbert Bindley, *The Oecumenical Documents of the Faith* (London, 1899), p. 17.

7. *De Decretis* 25.

8. *Letter to the Bishops of Egypt* 21.

9. *Oratio Contra Arianos* 1.1–10; *De Decretis,* passim.

10. On the role of the Bible in ecclesiastical controversy, see Jaroslav J. Pelikan, "Exegesis and the History of

Theology," in *Luther the Expositor* (St. Louis, 1959), pp. 5–31.

11. *Oratio contra Arianos* 2.18 ff.

12. *Ibid.* 2.65.

13. *Ibid.* 3.51.

14. Epistle 204 (trans. Roy J. Deferrari [Cambridge, 1961], III, 169).

15. Epistles 175 and 226 (trans. Deferrari, II, 457; III, 337–39); see also epp. 90 and 265.

16. C. H. Turner, *History and Use of Creeds and Anathemas*, p. 24, cited in J. N. D. Kelly, *Early Christian Creeds* (New York, ²1960, London ³1972), p. 205.

17. Epistle 39 (*Acta Conciliorum Oecumenicorum*), I, 1,1, p. 4, ll. 20–25.

18. On lists of citations from the fathers, see Marcel Richard, "Les Florilèges diphysites du Vᵉ et du VIᵉ siècle," in Aloys Grillmeier and Heinrich Bacht, *Das Konzil von Chalkedon* (Wuerzburg, 1951), pp. 721–48.

19. Jaroslav Pelikan, "Theology and Change," *Cross Currents* 19 (1969), p. 384.

## Chapter V

1. On the *Magdeburg Centuries*, see H. Scheible, *Die Entstehung der Magdeburger Zenturien. Ein Beitrag zur Geschichte der historiographischen Methode* ("Schriften des Vereins fuer Reformationsgeschichte," Nr. 183, Guetersloh, 1966); J. Massner, *Kirchliche Ueberlieferung und Autorität in Flacius-Kreis. Studien zu den Magdeburger Zenturien* (Berlin, 1964); P. Polman, "Flacius Illyricus, historien de l'Église," *Revue d'Histoire Ecclésiastique* 27 (1931), 27–73; also the sections in F. C. Baur, *Epochs*, pp. 81–105.

For Luther's views on church history, see most recently John M. Headley, *Luther's View of Church History* (New Haven, 1963).

2. Matthias Flacius, *Catalogus testium veritatis* (Frankfurt, 1666): "Vera Ecclesia ac Religio sunt perpetua, falsae vero Ecclesiae et Religiones subinde varie mutantur et transformantur. Iam ex omnibus scriptoribus et historiis constat, nostram Ecclesiam et Religionem, quae a Romano Pontifice dependet, esse valde antiquam, diuturnam, atque adeo in de a Christe et Apostolorum temporibus originem habere, ac veluti per traducem ordinariam re successionem propagatam esse. Vestra vero religio nova est. . . . Hoc sophisma vere quidem dissolvere atque destruere est perfacile negata perpetuitate adversariae doctrinae et Ecclesiae, item nostra novitatate." Preface, unnumbered pp. 1–2; Baur, p. 81, fn. 1.

3. *Historiae Ecclesiasticae* (Basel, 1624), Preface, p. 3a. "Nequaquam igitur articuli coelestis doctrinae variant, sed sunt huiusmodi."

4. *Corpus Reformatorum* (Frankfurt am Main, 1834–60), XI, 727 ff.; see Scheible, pp. 16–17.

5. *Hist. Eccles.* XI, 7 (Basel, 1624), p. 189c; Baur, *Epochs,* pp. 89–90.

6. Baur, *Epochs,* p. 96.

7. "Gratia similiter, quoties praecipuo Christi beneficio sermo est, significat passive, hoc est gratuitam benevolentiam et favorem solutionem a male dicto legis propter Christum et totius obedientiae impletionis legis, mereti, justitiae per sanguinem partae, ipsius videlicet Christi gratuitam imputationem." *Hist. Eccles.* I, 1,4, pp. 73–74; also pp. 86, 94.

8. *Annales Ecclesiastici auctore Caesare Baronio Sorano Novissima Editio* (Coloniae Agrippinae, 1624), pref.: "Praesertim contra *Novatores* nostri temporis," and "pro sacrarum traditionum antiquitate, ac S. Romanae Catholicae Ecclesiae potestate."
On the *Annales,* see Dictionnaire d'Histoire et de Géographie Ecclésiastiques (Paris, 1932), VI, 871 ff.; Baur, *Epochs,* pp. 106–16.

9. *Annales,* pref. p. 3; (Baur, *Epochs,* p. 108).

## Chapter VI

1. On the left wing of the Reformation, see George Huntston Williams, *The Radical Reformation* (Philadelphia, 1962). On the historiography of the radical reformation, see Peter Meinhold, *Geschichte der kirchlichen Historiographie* (Munich, 1967), I, 296 ff.; also Frank J. Wray, *History in the Eyes of Sixteenth Century Anabaptists* (Yale University Ph.D. dissertation, 1967).
2. *Pia Desideria*, by Philipp Jacob Spener, ed., trans. Theodore G. Tappert (Philadelphia, 1964), pp. 44–46.
3. *Ibid.*, p. 49.
4. Gottfried Arnold, *Unpartheyische Kirchen und Ketzer Historien vom Anfang des Neuen Testaments biss auf das Jahr Christi 1688* (Schaffhausen, 1740), 3 vols. On Arnold, see most recently Herman Doerries, *Geist und Geschichte bei Gottfried Arnold* (Goettingen, 1963); Baur, *Epochs*, pp. 116–33.
5. Arnold, *Kirchenhistorien*, I, 161 (Baur, p. 124; translation revised by author).
6. Arnold, I, 359 (Baur, p. 121).
7. See Baur, pp. 136 ff.; Meinhold, II, 11 ff.
8. Siegmund Jacob Baumgarten, *Evangelische Glaubenslehre*. Erster Band. Mit einigen Anmerkungen, Vorrede und historischen Einleitung herausgegeben von Johann Salomo Semler (Halle, 1764). See especially his comments on pp. 70–72, 84. Also his *Historiae Ecclesiasticae Selecta*, Tomus Primus (Halle, 1767), pp. 11–12.
9. *Johann Kiddels Abhandlung von der Eingebung der heiligen Schrift, mit vielen freiern Zusätzen von D. Johann Salomo Semler* (Halle, 1783), p. 150; cited in Baur, *Epochs*, p. 159.
10. Cited in Paul F. Boller, Jr., *American Thought in Transition: The Impact of Evolutionary Naturalism, 1865–1900* (Chicago, 1969), pp. 22, 24.

11. John Henry Newman, *An Essay on the Development of Christian Doctrine* (New York, Doubleday Image Books, 1960), pp. 37–41.
On Newman, see Owen Chadwick, *From Bossuet to Newman. The Idea of Doctrinal Development* (Cambridge, 1957).

12. *Essay,* p. 53.

13. *Essay,* pp. 59, 175, 177.

14. G. K. Chesterton, *St. Thomas Aquinas* (New York, 1956), p. 28.

15. Adolf von Harnack, *What is Christianity?,* trans. Thomas Bailey Saunders (Third, revised edition, London 1904, New York, Harper Torchbooks, 1957).

16. Adolf von Harnack, *History of Dogma,* trans. Neil Buchanan (New York, Dover Publications, 1961), I, 60.

17. *History of Dogma,* pp. 1, 15–17.

18. *Ibid.,* p. 22.

19. *Ibid.,* pp. 50, 72.

20. See Walter Glawe, *Die Hellenisierung des Christentums in der Geschichte der Theologie von Luther bis auf die Gegenwart* (Berlin, 1912).

21. Adolf von Harnack, *Lehrbuch der Dogmengeschichte* (Tuebingen, 1931[5]), I, 14 (my translation).

22. *History of Dogma,* I, 40.

23. John H. Elliott, "The New Testament is Catholic; a re-evaluation of sola Scriptura," *Una Sancta* 23 (1966), p. 4; also his "A Catholic Gospel: Reflections on 'Early Catholicism' in the New Testament," *Catholic Biblical Quarterly* 31 (1969), pp. 212–23.

24. Ernst Kaesemann, "Ministry and Community in the New Testament," *Essays on New Testament Themes* (London, 1964), pp. 75–76.

25. *Ibid.,* pp. 78 ff.

26. *Ibid.,* pp. 85–89.

27. *Ibid.,* p. 85.

28. *Ibid.,* p. 93.

29. Elliott, pp. 10–11; Hans Küng, *Structures of the Church* (New York, 1964), p. 162.

## Chapter VII

1. On the theological problems raised by historical thinking, see Van A. Harvey, *The Historian and the Believer* (New York, 1966; London 1967).
2. On the apostolic fathers, see Robert M. Grant, *The Apostolic Fathers* (New York, 1964).
3. See Walter Bauer, *Rechtglaeubigkeit und Ketzerei im aeltesten Christentum* (Tuebingen, 1964); translation to appear at Fortress Press in near future; also Helmut Koester, "Gnomai Diaphoroi, The Origin and Nature of Diversification in the History of Early Christianity," *Harvard Theological Review*, 58 (1965), pp. 279–318.
4. See especially Reginald Fuller, *The Foundations of New Testament Christology* (London, 1965); Ferdinand Hahn, *Christologische Hoheitstitel. Ihre Geschichte im frühen Christentum* (Goettingen, 1963).
5. Fuller, pp. 142 ff.
6. Fuller, pp. 203 ff.
7. Cited in G. R. G. Mure, *The Philosophy of Hegel* (London, 1965), p. 44.
8. Gerhard von Rad, *Old Testament Theology* (New York and Edinburgh 1962–65, I, 119.
9. Gerhard von Rad, II, 240.
10. Gerhard von Rad, II, 319.
11. Gerhard von Rad, II, 45–46.
12. Origen, *Contra Celsum* 3.55 (trans. and ed. H. Chadwick [Cambridge, 1953], pp. 165–66); see also 1.9.
13. Gustave Bardy, " 'Philosophie' et 'philosophe' dans le vocabulaire chrétien des premières siècles," *Revue d'Ascétique et de Mystique* XXV (1949), pp. 97–108.
    See also Robert L. Wilken, "Towards a Social Interpretation of Early Christian Apologetics," *Church History* 39 (1970).
14. Origen, *Contra Celsum* 1.64; 8.76.

15. On the significance of Nicaea in the history of Christian thought, see most recently Friedo Ricken, "Nikaia als Krisis des altkirchlichen Platonismus," *Theologie und Philosophie* 44 (1969), pp. 321–41, and the extensive bibliography cited there.

The discussion of the Trinity led to another "innovation" within Christian thought. In a study of Gregory of Nyssa, Ekkehard Muehlenberg has shown how Gregory of Nyssa formulated a new conception of the nature of God as a result of his controversy with Eunomius, a second-generation Arian. Traditionally, Christians expressed God's transcendence by such ideas as God as source, origin, beginning of all things, as had the Greeks. One way of saying the same thing in Christian language was to call God "unbegotten" (*agenetos*). But if the Son was "begotten," he could not be God. Gregory argued, in response to these views, that unbegottenness was not the chief defining characteristic of the deity, but infinity, that is, boundlessness. If this is so, then it is possible to speak of the Son as truly God, even though he was begotten of the Father. In making infinity the primary conception for God, Gregory not only went beyond early Christian thinkers, e.g. Origen (see his *De Principiis* 2.9.1), but he introduced a new conception that had no precedent in any thinker in Greek antiquity. Gregory's new idea was possible because of the confrontation of Greek *and* Christian thinking. See Ekkehard Muehlenberg, *Die Unendlichkeit Gottes bei Gregor von Nyssa* (Goettingen, 1966).

## Chapter VIII

1. Albert Outler, *Christian Tradition and the Unity We Seek* (New York, 1957), p. 51.
2. See the comments of Charles Norris Cochrane, *Christianity and Classical Culture* (New York, 1957), on the idealizing of the past in ancient Rome. Livy's idealized

portrait of early Rome in the preface to his history "involve[s] a claim that it is both desirable and possible to erect a future upon the basis of an idealized past. Such a claim is, however, utterly unrealistic. In the first place, it ignores the truth that history does not repeat itself; that ever-changing situations constitute a perpetual challenge to the ingenuity and endurance of mankind. In the second, it presupposes that men are in fact at liberty to choose between perfectly arbitrary and abstract alternatives of 'vice' and 'virtue'; in other words, that there is nothing to prevent them, should they so desire, from living the life of their own grandfathers, the 'valiant men of old.' But this presupposition is wholly fallacious; since it implies that human beings stand in no essential or intrinsic relationship to social reality which, in point of fact, they themselves actually constitute." (pp. 96–97)

3. Rudolf Bultmann, *History and Eschatology* (Edinburgh, 1957), p. 120.
4. Wolfhart Pannenberg, *Theology and the Kingdom of God* (Philadelphia, 1969), pp. 114–15.
5. See chapter 1, note 8.
6. On the Christian reaction to Charles Y. Glock and Rodney Stark, *Christian Beliefs and Anti-Semitism* (New York, 1966), see Richard John Neuhaus, "Christian Belief, Anti-Semitism, and Salvation History," *Una Sancta* 23 (1966), pp. 72–81.
7. On history as "indicative," see Philip J. Jefner, *Faith and the Vitalities of History* (New York, 1966), pp. 9 ff., 70 ff., 80 ff.
8. The story can be found in *Baba Mezia* 596 (ed. I. Epstein, London, 1935), p. 353.

## Epilogue

1. Gregory of Nyssa, *Commentarius in Canticum Canticorum* (5:2), Oratio XI (ed. Jaeger, Leiden, 1960, VI, p. 321); trans. Herbert Musurillo and Jean Daniélou, *From Glory to Glory* (New York, 1961), pp. 245–46.